SAP Lumira Essentials

Discover how to make your business data more interactive and engaging with SAP Lumira

Dmitry Anoshin

BIRMINGHAM - MUMBAI

SAP Lumira Essentials

First published: September 2015

Production reference: 1260815

Published by Packt Publishing Ltd.
Livery Place
35 Livery Street
Birmingham B3 2PB, UK.

ISBN 978-1-78528-181-5

www.packtpub.com

Credits

Author
Dmitry Anoshin

Reviewers
Ahmad Abdel Mouti Assaf
Vitaliy Rudnytskiy
Arjun Srinivasan
Gang Tao

Commissioning Editor
Dipika Gaonkar

Acquisition Editor
Reshma Raman

Content Development Editor
Anish Sukumaran

Technical Editor
Siddhesh Patil

Copy Editors
Relin Hedly
Sonia Mathur

Project Coordinator
Izzat Contractor

Proofreader
Safis Editing

Indexer
Monica Ajmera Mehta

Graphics
Disha Haria

Production Coordinator
Conidon Miranda

Cover Work
Conidon Miranda

About the Author

Dmitry Anoshin is a data-centric technologist and a recognized expert in building and implementing business/digital analytics solutions. He has a successful track record when it comes to implementing business and digital intelligence projects in numerous industries, including retail, finance, marketing, and e-commerce.

Dmitry possesses in-depth knowledge of digital/business intelligence, ETL, data warehousing, and big data technologies. He has extensive experience in the data integration process and is proficient in using various data warehousing methodologies. Dmitry constantly exceeds project expectations when he works for financial, machine tool, and retail industries.

He has completed a number of multinational full BI/DI solution life cycle implementation projects. With expertise in data modeling, Dmitry also has a background and business experience in multiple relation databases, OLAP systems, and NoSQL databases.

He has a technical blog at `http://techbusinessintelligence.blogspot.ru/` and publishes his presentations at `http://www.slideshare.net/dimoobraznii`.

In addition, he has reviewed the following books for Packt Publishing:

- *SAP BusinessObjects Reporting Cookbook*
- *Creating Universes with SAP BusinessObjects*
- *Learning SAP BusinessObjects Dashboards*

I'd like to thank my wife, Svetlana, my daughter, Anna, and my son, Vasily, for their love and support. I love you all very much.

About the Reviewers

Ahmad Abdel Mouti Assaf holds a PhD degree in computer science and specializes in semantic web and information retrieval from Telecom ParisTech. Before moving on to start a new venture with a start-up in London, he worked with the business intelligence team of SAP Labs, France. His work revolved around enabling smart workflows and the semantic enrichment of data in SAP HANA and Lumira.

In his spare time, he likes to toy with web development technologies, such as Node.js (JavaScript), Python, PHP, and so on. You can find more information about Ahmad at http://ahmadassaf.com.

Vitaliy Rudnytskiy is a principal architect at SAP, where he is involved in building SAP Developer Center (http://developers.sap.com). His main interests lie in big data and fast data solutions, analytics, and data visualizations. Vitaliy graduated from the University of Technologies in Wrocław, Poland. Before joining SAP, he spent 10 years as a technology consultant in the U.S. and Europe. Vitaliy's work has been published in various industry magazines. He writes on his blog (Vital BI) and has been a speaker at multiple conferences on both sides of the Atlantic. In 2010, he was nominated and selected as a member of the prestigious group of SAP Mentors (http://sapmentors.sap.com), the community of top influencers in the SAP ecosystem. You can reach him on Twitter and GitHub at @Sygyzmundovych.

Arjun Srinivasan is a graduate student pursuing computer science at the Georgia Institute of Technology in Atlanta, GA (USA). His primary research includes understanding how the techniques from visual analytics, information visualization, and machine learning can be leveraged effectively in the domains of business intelligence, product intelligence, and intelligence analysis. Arjun has previously worked at SAP Labs India. He has given multiple presentations on SAP Lumira and how it can be used by students in particular. To read more about his research and presentations, you can visit `http://arjun010.github.io/`.

Gang Tao is an experienced software architect with experience in the business intelligence, data visualization, and ERP domains. He is currently a software architect working on data acquisition for the big data platform. Gang has more than 15 years of experience in developing software for different domains. He graduated from Beijing University of Posts and Telecommunications and holds a master's degree in telecommunication network management.

Previously, he has worked at SAP and EMC and is currently working at Splunk.

I'd like to thank my wife, Vivian, and my daughter, Yoyo, for their constant support. They always motivated and encouraged me when there was a problem I could not solve.

www.PacktPub.com

Support files, eBooks, discount offers, and more

For support files and downloads related to your book, please visit www.PacktPub.com.

Did you know that Packt offers eBook versions of every book published, with PDF and ePub files available? You can upgrade to the eBook version at www.PacktPub.com and as a print book customer, you are entitled to a discount on the eBook copy. Get in touch with us at service@packtpub.com for more details.

At www.PacktPub.com, you can also read a collection of free technical articles, sign up for a range of free newsletters and receive exclusive discounts and offers on Packt books and eBooks.

https://www2.packtpub.com/books/subscription/packtlib

Do you need instant solutions to your IT questions? PacktLib is Packt's online digital book library. Here, you can search, access, and read Packt's entire library of books.

Why subscribe?

- Fully searchable across every book published by Packt
- Copy and paste, print, and bookmark content
- On demand and accessible via a web browser

Free access for Packt account holders

If you have an account with Packt at www.PacktPub.com, you can use this to access PacktLib today and view 9 entirely free books. Simply use your login credentials for immediate access.

Table of Contents

Preface

With the increasing popularity of data discovery, self-service BI, and visualizations around the world, more and more tools are being developed for data discovery, which allows you to eliminate the complexities of analyzing and discovering data. You can learn the techniques of data discovery, build amazing visualizations, create fantastic stories, and share these visualizations through electronic mediums with one of the most powerful tools: SAP Lumira. Moreover, this book will focus on extracting data from different sources, such as plain text, Microsoft Excel spreadsheets, the SAP BusinessObjects BI platform, SAP HANA, and SQL databases. Finally, it will teach you how to publish the result of your painstaking work on various mediums, such as SAP BI Clients, SAP Lumira Cloud, and so on. This book provides you with a step-by-step guide and discusses the essentials of SAP Lumira, starting with an overview of SAP Lumira family of products. This book demonstrates various data discovery techniques using real-world scenarios of an online e-commerce retailer. Moreover, this book will provide you with detailed recipes of installations, administration, and customizations of SAP Lumira. In addition, it shows you how to work with data, starting from acquiring data from various data sources to preparing and visualizing it through the rich functionalities of SAP Lumira. Finally, it teaches you how to present data via a data story or infographic and publish it across your organization or World Wide Web.

What this book covers

Chapter 1, *Meeting SAP Lumira*, talks about SAP Lumira, a powerful data discovery tool for end users. In this chapter, you will learn about SAP Lumira and the different data discovery processes, in addition to the SAP Lumira interface. It also teaches you how to deploy SAP Lumira on your computer. It also provides real-world examples, which will help you to learn the essentials of SAP Lumira.

Chapter 2, Connecting to Data Sources, explains the various data sources that hold valuable data. It provides information on the different kinds of data sources you can discover and how to use them with SAP Lumira data connectors.

Chapter 3, Preparing Data, takes you through the various techniques of data preparation, such as cleaning, filtering, formatting, enriching, and merging.

Chapter 4, Visualizing Data and Telling Stories with It, tells you how to discover data and create amazing visualizations based on your data. It teaches you how to tell a story with your data so that it is clear and interesting for everyone. SAP Lumira provides you the opportunity to build an infographic based on your data. It allows you to share data visualization, datasets, and data stories through various channels easily.

Chapter 5, Rocking Your Data in the Sky - SAP Lumira Cloud, gives you information about SAP Lumira Cloud. The leaders of the IT industry build clouds and move their applications to the cloud, which gives fantastic flexibility and performance. SAP Lumira isn't an exception. This chapter takes a look at SAP Lumira Cloud and explores the basic functionality of the cloud solution.

Chapter 6, Administrating and Customizing SAP Lumira, provides information about the management of SAP Lumira. SAP Lumira provides you the opportunity to extend the rich functionality of a tool using the customization of an SDK. It teaches you how to create a custom data visualization and acquire basic knowledge about the SAP Lumira SDK.

Chapter 7, Connecting to SAP BusinessObjects BI Platform and SAP HANA, extends the SAP BIP functionality with rich data visualization and the discovery functionality of SAP Lumira. It also teaches you how to use SAP HANA as a data source for data visualization and learn some useful techniques about how to handle it with extremely large datasets of SAP HANA.

What you need for this book

In order to start learning SAP Lumira and the techniques of data discovery, you need to have a passion for analytics software, data visualization, and new technologies. In addition, you should have access to the Internet so that you can download the SAP Lumira desktop and content for this book. SAP Lumira is a Windows-based application, and if you have a computer that runs an operation system other than Windows, you can use the virtual machine to run SAP Lumira on it.

Who this book is for

If you are a SAP user, business analyst, BI developer, or even a junior data engineer who discovers data, then this book is exactly what you are looking for. Hands-on practical examples, real-world solutions, and best practices make this book an essential guide to learn a new tool to build creative visualizations using SAP Lumira. Clear a space on your desk and get ready to become a data geek.

Conventions

In this book, you will find a number of styles of text that distinguish between different kinds of information. Here are some examples of these styles, and an explanation of their meaning.

Code words in text, database table names, folder names, filenames, file extensions, pathnames, dummy URLs, user input, and Twitter handles are shown as follows: "In text pad just type:

```
InstallDir=C:\Program Files\SAP Lumira\."
```

A block of code is set as follows:

```
select count(*) from dim_dates;
select count(*) from dim_orders;
select count(*) from dim_products;
```

New terms and **important words** are shown in bold. Words that you see on the screen, in menus or dialog boxes for example, appear in the text like this: "Find distributive and double click on **SAPLumirainstall.exe**".

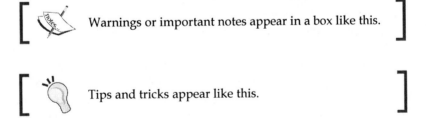

Warnings or important notes appear in a box like this.

Tips and tricks appear like this.

Reader feedback

Feedback from our readers is always welcome. Let us know what you think about this book—what you liked or may have disliked. Reader feedback is important for us to develop titles that you really get the most out of.

To send us general feedback, simply send an e-mail to feedback@packtpub.com, and mention the book title via the subject of your message.

If there is a topic that you have expertise in and you are interested in either writing or contributing to a book, see our author guide on www.packtpub.com/authors.

Customer support

Now that you are the proud owner of a Packt book, we have a number of things to help you to get the most from your purchase.

Downloading the example code

You can download the example code files for all Packt books you have purchased from your account at http://www.packtpub.com. If you purchased this book elsewhere, you can visit http://www.packtpub.com/support and register to have the files e-mailed directly to you.

Errata

Although we have taken every care to ensure the accuracy of our content, mistakes do happen. If you find a mistake in one of our books—maybe a mistake in the text or the code—we would be grateful if you would report this to us. By doing so, you can save other readers from frustration and help us improve subsequent versions of this book. If you find any errata, please report them by visiting http://www.packtpub.com/submit-errata, selecting your book, clicking on the **errata submission form** link, and entering the details of your errata. Once your errata are verified, your submission will be accepted and the errata will be uploaded on our website, or added to any list of existing errata, under the Errata section of that title. Any existing errata can be viewed by selecting your title from http://www.packtpub.com/support.

Piracy

Piracy of copyright material on the Internet is an ongoing problem across all media. At Packt, we take the protection of our copyright and licenses very seriously. If you come across any illegal copies of our works, in any form, on the Internet, please provide us with the location address or website name immediately so that we can pursue a remedy.

Please contact us at copyright@packtpub.com with a link to the suspected pirated material.

We appreciate your help in protecting our authors, and our ability to bring you valuable content.

Questions

You can contact us at questions@packtpub.com if you are having a problem with any aspect of the book, and we will do our best to address it.

1
Meeting SAP Lumira

Before getting started with SAP Lumira, you need to learn about data discovery. Maybe this term is not new to you, however, we need to clarify what it is in the case of SAP Lumira. In addition, it will be interesting and useful to learn some of the theory.

In this chapter you will learn:

- What data discovery is, and how it complements a traditional data warehouse (DWH) and business intelligence (BI)
- Data discovery terms
- Common organizational architecture and the role of data discovery in the organization
- We meet with one of the most powerful and flexible data discovery tools – SAP Lumira
- We meet *Unicorn Fashion, an* e-commerce retail company

Big data analytics

We are living in a century of information technology. There are a lot of electronic devices around us which generate lots of data. For example, you can surf the Internet, visit a couple of news portals, order new Nike Air Max shoes from a web store, write a couple of messages to your friend, and chat on Facebook. Your every action produces data. We can multiply that action by the amount of people who have access to the internet or just use a cell phone, and we get really BIG DATA. Of course, you have a question: how big is it? Now, it starts from *terabytes* or even *petabytes*. The volume is not the only issue; moreover, we struggle with the variety of data. As a result, it is not enough to analyze only the structured data. We should dive deep in to unstructured data, such as machine data which are generated by various machines.

Nowadays, we should have a new core competence—dealing with big data—, because these vast data volumes won't be just stored, they need to be analysed and mined for information that management can use in order to make right business decisions. This helps to make the business more competitive and efficient.

Unfortunately, in modern organizations there are still many manual steps needed in order to get data and try to answer your business questions. You need the help of your IT guys, or need to wait until new data is available in your enterprise data warehouse. In addition, you are often working with an inflexible BI tool, which can only refresh a report or export it in to Excel. You definitely need a new approach, which gives you a competitive advantage, dramatically reduces errors, and accelerates business decisions.

So, we can highlight some of the key points for this kind of analytics:

- Integrating data from heterogeneous systems
- Giving more access to data
- Using sophisticated analytics
- Reducing manual coding
- Simplifying processes
- Reducing time to prepare data
- Focusing on self-service
- Leveraging powerful computing resources

We could continue this list with many other bullet points.

If you are a fan of traditional BI tools (later in this chapter, we will compare BI and data discovery tools), you may think that it is almost impossible. Yes, you are right, it is impossible. That's why we need to change the rules of the game. As the business world changes, you must change as well.

Maybe you have guessed what this means, but if not, I can help you. In this book, I will focus on a new approach of doing data analytics, which is more flexible and powerful. It is called data discovery. Of course, we need the right way in order to overcome all the challenges of the modern world. That's why we have chosen SAP Lumira—one of the most powerful data discovery tools in the modern market. But before diving deep into this amazing tool, let's consider some of the challenges of data discovery that are in our path, as well as data discovery advantages.

Data discovery challenges

Let's imagine that you have several terabytes of data. Unfortunately, it is raw unstructured data. In order to get business insight from this data you have to spend a lot of time in order to prepare and clean the data. In addition, you are restricted by the capabilities of your machine. That's why a good data discovery tool usually is combined of software and hardware. As a result, this gives you more power for exploratory data analysis.

Let's imagine that this entire big data store is in Hadoop or any NoSQL data store. You have to at least be at good programmer in order to do analytics on this data. Here we can find other benefit of a good data discovery tool: it gives a powerful tool to business users, who are not as technical and maybe don't even know SQL.

Apache Hadoop is an open source software project that enables distributed processing of large data sets across clusters of commodity servers. It is designed to scale up from a single server to thousands of machines, with a very high degree of fault tolerance. Rather than relying on high-end hardware, the resilience of these clusters comes from the software's ability to detect and handle failures at the application layer.

A NoSQL data store is a next generation database, mostly addressing some of the following points: non-relational, distributed, open-source, and horizontally scalable.

Data discovery versus business intelligence

You may be confused about data discovery and business intelligence technologies; it seems they are very close to each other or even BI tools can do all what data discovery can do. And why do we need a separate data discovery tool, such as, SAP Lumira?

In order to better understand the difference between the two technologies, you can look at the table below:

	Enterprise BI	Data discovery
Key users	All users	Advanced analysts
Approach	Vertically-oriented (top to bottom), semantic layers, requests to existing repositories	Vertically-oriented (bottom-up), mushup, putting data in the selected repository
Interface	Reports, dashboards	Visualization
Users	Reporting	Analysis
Implementation	By IT consultants	By business users

Let's consider the pros and cons of data discovery:

Pros:

- Rapidly analyze data with a short shelf life
- Ideal for small teams
- Best for tactical analysis
- Great for answering on-off questions quickly

Cons:

- Difficult to handle for enterprise organizations
- Difficult for junior users
- Lack of scalability

As a result, it is clear that BI and data discovery handles their own tasks and complement each other.

The role of data discovery

Most organizations have a data warehouse. It was planned to supporting daily operations and to help make business decisions. But sometimes organizations need to meet new challenges. For example, *Retail Company* wants to improve their customer experience and decide to work closely with the customer database. Analysts try to segment customers into cohorts and try to analyse customer's behavior. They need to handle all customer data, which is quite big. In addition, they can use external data in order to learn more about their customers. If they start to use a corporate BI tool, every interaction, such as adding new a field or filter, can take 10-30 minutes. Another issue is adding a new field to an existing report. Usually, it is impossible without the help of IT staff, due to security or the complexities of the BI Enterprise solution. This is unacceptable in a modern business. Analysts want get an answer to their business questions immediately, and they prefer to visualize data because, as you know, human perception of visualization is much higher than text. In addition, these analysts may be independent from IT. They have their data discovery tool and they can connect to any data sources in the organization and check their crazy hypotheses.

There are hundreds of examples where BI and DWH is weak, and data discovery is strong.

Data discovery for your business

Let's discuss the various possible users of the data discovery tool and their advantages. Here's a small schema of possible data flows in an organization:

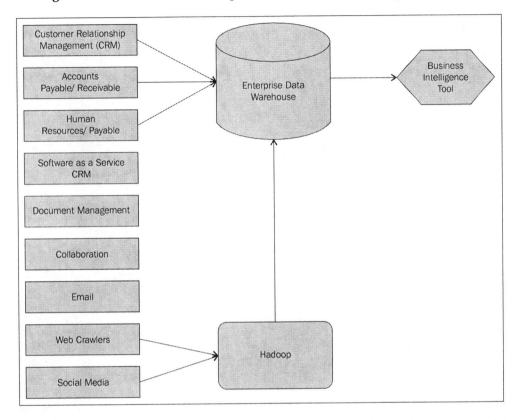

There are many systems which generate data. Organizations try to catch all the data and put it in data warehouse. In addition, for big data volumes they can use Hadoop because it offers cheap storage, high scalability, distributed computing power, and can be used as a staging area for raw data.

On top of the DWH we have a business intelligence tool, such as SAP BusinessObjects, MicroStrategy, Oracle BI, or Cognos BI. This uses data from the DWH and gives the opportunity to build reports and visualize data. But it takes long a time to create the semantic layer via a BI tool such as the universe, schema or repository. In addition, it requires technical skills. As a result, there is no agility and it is not user friendly for any non technical business users.

Fortunately, we have a data discovery tool which can easily complement our existing BI tool. Let's look and compare how a data discovery tool can impact on our data flow in an organization:

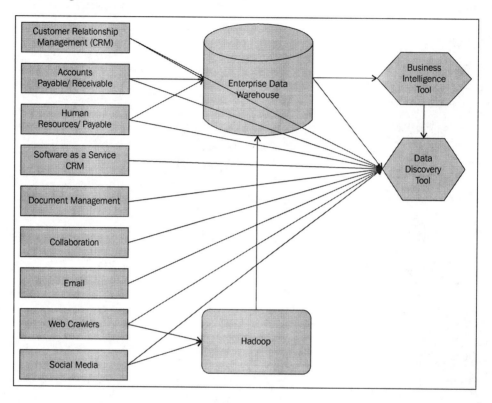

Data discovery tools have many advantages for the whole organization. It can be easy to connect with various data sources, and it doesn't require any technical skills from the business users. Users can combine and merge various data sources and visualize big data sets. They can easily find insights from data and use it for their decision making process.

In addition, let's now look at the benefits of using a data discovery tool for various roles in the organization:

- **Business management**: It provides better information for the decision process, plus greater accuracy, richer detail, an enhanced ability to identify factors affecting business outcomes, and the connections among them.

- **IT managers**: It eliminates the stream of individual support requests for analytics. It will free IT staff for other responsibilities and improves internal customer satisfaction.

- **IT staff**: It allows them to dispense with the oodles of requests for data extracts.

- **Distinguished analysts**: It gives greater productivity, fewer errors, and more time to spend on the more interesting aspects of data analysis. It allows better and easier data access, better integration among data sources, and the opportunity to probe data in greater detail. It provides a roader range of analytical methods.

- **Other data analysis roles**: It provides access to a greater variety and depth of data, and to analysis methods.

- **Everybody else**: It provides better information to support daily decision making at all levels of the organization.

We can continue this list with other roles in your organization and try to determine, what benefits they will get.

Data discovery best practices

In my work, I use data discovery quite often, and I want to highlight some useful best practices:

- **Agility and rapid cycle iteration**: It gives you the opportunity to rapidly discover any set of data and very quickly try a new hypothesis. In any case where the new hypothesis fails, you can quickly start with another new one.

- **Begin with the end in mind**: Even if you don't know what you should do to find something in a particular data set, you can start to explore the data and get business insight. But it is highly recommended that you try to understand the business process.

- **Take advantages of data insights**: During data exploration you may find valuable new information, for example, if you recognize a burst of high-volume sales for a new product. Immediately you can dive deep, and, for example, look to answer the question of, who is buying this product. We can dive deeper and try to understand more and more. Finally, we can create a new marketing segment based on your valuable insights.

Introducing SAP Lumira

Starting from this point, we will focus on learning SAP Lumira. First of all, we need to understand what SAP Lumira is exactly.

SAP Lumira is a family of data discovery tools which give us an opportunity to create amazing visualizations or even tell fantastic stories based on our big or small data. We can connect most of the popular data sources, such as **Relational Database Management Systems (RDBMSs)**, flat files, excel spreadsheets or SAP applications. We are able to create datasets with measures, dimensions, hierarchies, or variables. In addition, Lumira allows us to prepare, edit, and clean our data before it is processed.

SAP Lumira offers us a huge arsenal of graphical charts and tables to visualize our data. In addition, we can create data stories or even infographics based on our data by grouping charts, single cells, or tables together on boards to create presentation-style dashboards. Moreover, we can add images or text in order to add details.

The following are the three main products in the Lumira family offered by SAP:

- SAP Lumira Desktop
- SAP Lumira Server
- SAP Lumira Cloud

Lumira Desktop can be either a personal edition or a standard edition. Both of them give you the opportunity to analyse data on your local machine. You can even share your visualizations or insights via PDF or XLS.

Lumira Server is also in two variations—*Edge* and *Server*. As you know, SAP BusinessObjects also has two types of license for the same software, Edge and Enterprise, and they differ only in terms of the number of users and the type of license. The Edge version is smaller; for example, it can cover the needs of a team or even the whole department.

Lumira Cloud is **Software as a Service (SaaS)**. It helps to quickly visualize large volumes of data without having to sacrifice performance or security. It is especially designed to speed time to insight. In addition, it saves time and money with flexible licensing options.

Here is a table which will help you to compare the various versions of SAP Lumira and choose the best one for your purposes:

	Desktop		Server		Cloud
	Personal	Standard	Edge	Enterprise	Cloud
Access XLSX and CSV files	+		+	+	+
Access databases		+	+	+	
Access SAP HANA and BI universes		+	+	+	
Combine and transform data	+	+	+	+	
Create visualizations, boards, and infographics	+	+	+	+	+
Secure sharing			+	+	+
Web / mobile support			+	+	+
Free edition/ trial	+	+	+	+	+

The dataset, and its charts, that you create in SAP Lumira Desktop are saved in documents with the file format .lums. This is a document that contains a zipped archive with the data source connection information, the data definition and data, and the visualizations.

Getting SAP Lumira

Since we now have an idea what SAP Lumira is and how it can help us with data discovery or big data analytics, lets download and install SAP Lumira. In addition, we will also learn a bit about Lumira's nice, friendly interface. In this book, we will use the SAP Lumira Standard edition; you can download it with a trial key for a 60 days trial.

There are three methods for getting SAP Lumira:

- Download it from `http://www.saplumira.com`
- Download it from `http://support.sap.com/swdc`
- Download from `https://www.packtpub.com/support`

  This is the best choice because most of the books were written based on SAP Lumira Desktop version 1.21. It is possible to use the last version of SAP Lumira, which is very similar to its previous versions, but it can have some changes in design.

Before downloading and installing lets have a look at the system requirements of SAP Lumira:

Operating System	32-bit	64-bit
Windows 7 SP1	+	+
Windows Server 2008 R2SP1	N/A	+
Windows 8 / Windows 8.1	Not supported	+
Windows Server 2012 / Windows Server 2012 R2	N/A	+

The following table explains the hardware requirements:

Hardware requirements	32-bit	64-bit
RAM (minimum)	2 GB	3 GB
RAM (recommended)	4 GB	
Screen resolution (minimum)	1280 x 720	
Free hard disk space needed for installation	3.7 GB	
Open local ports	Local port 6401 should be open and you need at least one open local port in the port range: 4520-4539	

If your machine complies with these requirements, you can download it from `http://saplumira.com/download/`. In my case, I chose *Free Download (64-bit)*.

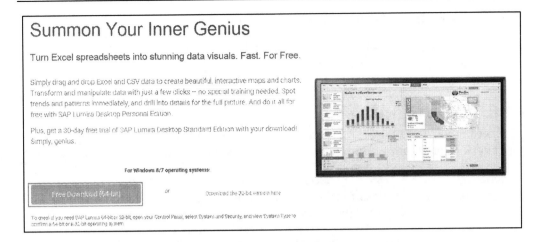

After downloading SAP Lumira, we are going to install it.

Installing SAP Lumira

You have just completed the first step in the amazing world of data discovery. You know a little bit about why we need data discovery, and you just downloaded the software which gives you outstanding capabilities to explore data and become a data geek.

First of all, we need to install SAP Lumira. There are two ways to accomplish this task:

- Installing SAP Lumira with the wizard
- Silent installation

The installation wizard

I prefer using the wizard, but you can also go ahead with a silent installation, if you wish. We will see how to do it later in this chapter.

In order to run the wizard:

1. Find distributive and double click on **SAPLumirainstall.exe**.
2. Enter a destination folder, for example `C:\Program Files\SAP Lumira\`, and click **Next**.
3. Accept the license agreement and click **Next**.
4. Click **Next** and wait till the process finishes.

5. Click **Finish** and mark **Launch SAP Lumira**.

You just successfully installed SAP Lumira and launched it. It is ready to work. But first, let's take a tour around the interface.

Silent installation

In a silent installation the SAP Lumira installation wizard runs without displaying a user interface or prompting for user input; it reads the required input from a text file.

A silent installation is typically used by system administrators to push multiple installations across an infrastructure. After creating a silent installation response file, you can add the silent-installation command to your installation script.

If you want to perform a silent installation, you should create a response file, which consists of two parameters:

- `<InstallDir>`—Then location where the SAP Lumira program files will be installed (required).
- `<userkeycode>`—License Key (optional).

In the text pad, just type:

```
InstallDir=C:\Program Files\SAP Lumira\
```

```
userkeycode=XXXXX-XX00000-XXXXXXX-XXXXXXX-XX2
```

Now we can start the silent installation:

1. Click **Start->Run** and enter `cmd` to open the **Run** window.
2. Navigate to, and double-click, the `SAPLumiraSetup.exe` self-extracting archive file.

   For example, the file might be located at `C:\Program Files\SAP Lumira\SAPLumiraSetup.exe`. Enter `SAPLumiraSetup.exe -s -r <ResponseFilePath>\response.ini`, where `<ResponseFilePath>` is the location where the response file will be saved. The parameter `-r` requires the file name and location of the response file you created. The optional parameter `-s` hides the self-extraction progress bar during a silent installation.

Getting familiar with the SAP Lumira interface

We have successfully installed SAP Lumira. Now we are going to get to know the user interface for Lumira. Go to **Start->All Programs->SAP Business Intelligence->SAP Lumira**.

SAP Lumira is a desktop application designed for acquiring, visualizing, and sharing data. The **Home** page of the application consists of four main areas, which have been marked in the following screenshot:

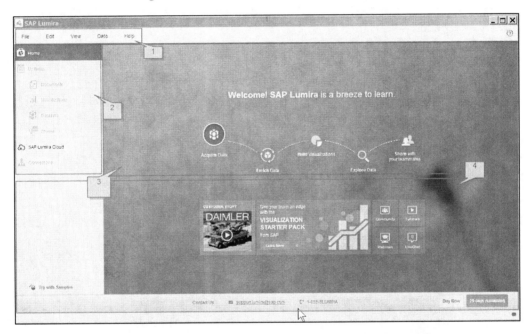

Let us take a look into each one of the 4 areas mentioned in the image:

- Menu Bar (**1**): As with most desktop applications, there's a menu bar at the top of the screen that is available on every page, which gives us access to the core features of the application, grouped in **File**, **Edit**, **View**, **Data,** and **Help** menus.

- Document (**2**): The document browser on the side enables quick access to the different types of items for which we can create a link to the SAP Lumira Cloud, and a list of the connections between documents and data sources. In addition, there is a **My Items** tab here, which use displays a list of all Lumira documents, **Visualizations**, **Datasets**, and **Stories**, which icons, labels, and subgroups to help distinguish between the different types.

- Homepage (**3**): The home page displays a graphic that outlines the main workflow within SAP Lumira. The **Acquire Data** icon is actually a button that provides a quick way to navigate to the screens for acquiring data and creating a new document.

- Bottom part of the homepage (**4**): At the bottom of the **Home** page, there are also links to samples, starter packs, communities, learning materials, and contacts.

SAP Lumira preferences

Before you start working with data, it is good to set the preferences. Lets go to **File->Preferences**:

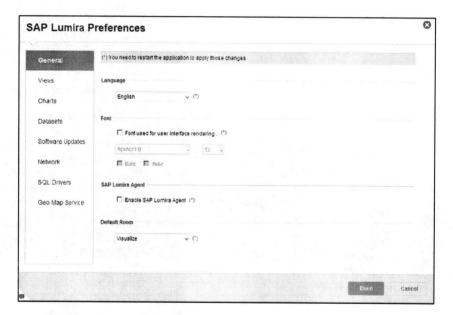

Using the file menu, we can open the **Preferences** dialog box to change the global settings for:

- Viewing the data
- Charting
- Enriching data sets
- Automating software updates
- Defining network connections

- Installing SQL drivers
- Enabling geo map services through Esri ArcGis Online (Esri needs a separate license)

Using these options, we can customize the SAP Lumira interface. If you are not sure what to change, you can just try to experiment with the settings.

Registering SAP Lumira

When we successfully finish installation of SAP Lumira, it will ask us to register the product. You can decline registration, but it will remind you each time, when you start the application.

You have the following registration options:

- Enter a key code
- Create a new SAP Lumira Cloud account
- Use an existing SAP Lumira Cloud account

We can also can use the personal edition, but you will be restricted to certain data source types only.

SAP Lumira license

SAP Lumira, as with other SAP products, is an enterprise solution. Despite the fact that it offers us a free personal edition of the software, this is not enough for all the capabilities which we want to learn. For example, we want to connect SAP BusinessObjects and SAP HANA, and we want to access databases because in real life most data is based in databases or in SAP applications.

We have several ways to get all capabilities of SAP Lumira:

- Use the 30 days trial version
- Buy a key
- Download a bundle of trial keys from `http://service.sap.com`

The first two points are self explanatory, but I would like to elaborate a bit on the third. Every quarter, SAP offers their customers temporary keys for most of the SAP Products, such as SAP BusinessObjects, SAP Data Services, and so on. It is funny, but many enterprise companies run their business based on these trial keys. It is forbidden to do it, so be careful because SAP can visit you with an audit at any time. But for home use it is fine.

In order to download temporary keys, as well as other SAP Software, you need *S-user*. This is an account for the SAP portal. You can ask for access to the SAP portal through your SAP manager, if your company runs SAP, or you can try asking the guys on the SAP forum.

 SAP S User ID is a unique number that SAP uses for identification of people on its web portals and databases. For example, you need an S User ID in order to access the SAP support portal or register for SAP certification. In this way, the S User ID is very similar to forms of authentication used by other large IT companies.

If you are a happy guy who has an S-user ID, I will show you how to download your bundle of trial keys:

1. Go to http://service.sap.com/support and log in to the portal using your S-user ID and password.

2. On the **Home** Page you will find the menu:

- ° **Help & Support**: Here, you can search SAP notes about various errors or software issues. In addition, you can create a new ticket for the SAP support team; this is only available, if your company bought SAP support.

- ° **Software Downloads**: This allows you you to search for SAP software and download it. In addition, you can find updates and service packs.

- ° **Keys & Requests**: This is our menu, where we can find temporary keys.

- ° **Release & Upgrade Info**: This is where you can find useful information about new versions of products.

All other menus are not that useful and we can miss them.

1. Click on **Keys & Requests**.
2. In the new window find **Temporary key** and click on it.
3. It will open a new window, and ask you to log in again. Keep calm, this is SAP.
4. Finally, it gives you the list of keys in PDF format.
5. Open the file and find the Lumira key in **Section 1**. Copy it.
6. Open the SAP Lumira application and go to **Help->Enter Code**. Paste the code.

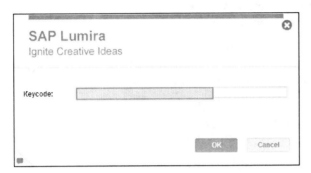

We have activated SAP Lumira, and we are ready to explore the data and learn SAP Lumira. But, before we start, we should meet with one fake ecommerce retailer.

Unicorn Fashion

I have decided to demonstrate all of the capabilities of SAP Lumira through real-world cases. For this purpose, I came up with an e-commerce retailer—*Unicorn Fashion*.

This is an extremely fast growing ecommerce retailer, operating in Manitoba, Canada. It has headquarters in Winnipeg. There are more than 100 employees who work at Unicorn, in various departments. Unicorn is a good example of a data driven company. Every decision is based on data analysis. It is one of the key factors of its success. There are lots of departments that use corporate data for analysis:

- **Human resources**: They analyse data for the employers, measure KPIs, and calculate bonuses and salaries
- **Top management**: They use daily dashboards and analyse sales trends. Their business decisions, based on data
- **Inventory**: They analyse prices, sizes, and brand. In addition, they calculate discounts for unpopular goods
- **Purchasing department**: Their category managers analyse how to get their brands to perform and try to plan capacity for the next season
- **Marketing department**: They plan, analyse, and measure marketing campaigns, and calculate marketing costs
- **Logistic department**: They analyse the performance of various logistic companies, to try to reduce costs, and calculate the bonus for the couriers
- **Finance department**: They calculate financial waterfall and main financial KPIs
- **Warehouse**: They measure KPIs and plan capacity

In terms of software, Unicorn mostly uses SAP technologies. For example, their main BI tool is SAP BusinessObjects. And they use various data sources as a DWH, such as Teradata and SAP HANA. In addition, Unicorn analysts like to connect OLTP systems and grab some transactional data in order to make quick decisions.

Through out this book, we will help unicorn staff to get the maximum value from their data. For this purpose. we will learn about SAP Lumira and try to figure out how it can be used in your organization or just in daily work.

Summary

In this chapter we have looked at data discovery. You have learnt what data discovery is and why is it useful. In addition, we compared data discovery with traditional business intelligence in order to highlight the pros and cons of each technology. Moreover, we have successfully installed SAP Lumira on our machine and discussed various versions of SAP Lumira and types of registration. In addition, we have touched of the SAP Lumira interface and learnt about the **Home** menu. Finally, we met the Unicorn Fashion company. In the next chapter, we will start working with data more closely. Through exercises, we will connect to various data sources such as flat files, databases, and so on.

Connecting to Data Sources

In this chapter, we will begin by talking about data sources which can provide data for SAP Lumira. Even in an ordinary organization we can find lots of data sources, such as **Enterprise Resource Planning (ERP)** systems, various **Online Transactional Processing (OLTP)** systems, which are based on relational databases, as well as corporate data warehouse (DWH). In addition, we will cover common files such as CSV, XLS or TXT.

It is not a secret that SAP as any other vendor, tries to build its own ecosystem, and SAP Lumira has its own place in this ecosystem, such as data discovery tool. As a result, users can easily connect their SAP BusinessObjects universes, SAP HANA, or publish visualizations in SAP BusinessObjects Explorer.

Therefore, we can be sure that SAP Lumira can cover all our needs by ingesting our data via a number of connections.

In this chapter the reader will learn:

- About DWH of Unicorn Fashion
- How to extract data from a corporate DWH using SQL Query, and how to configure a database connection
- How to connect a flat file
- Which SAP applications can be used with SAP Lumira

Downloading the example code

You can download the example code files for all Packt books you have purchased from your account at http://www.packtpub.com. If you purchased this book elsewhere, you can visit http://www.packtpub.com/support and register to have the files e-mailed directly to you.

Data connectors

In the previous chapter, we met SAP Lumira for the first time and we played with the interface, and the reader could adjust the general settings of SAP Lumira. In addition, we can find this interesting menu in the middle of the window:

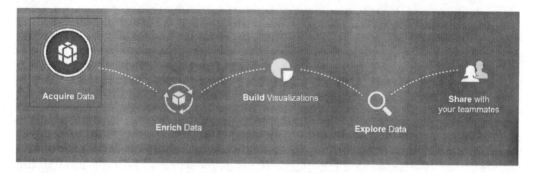

There are several steps which help us to discover our data and gain business insights. In this chapter we start from first step by exploring data in SAP Lumira to create a document and acquire a dataset, which can include part or all of the original values from a data source. This is through **Acquire Data**. Let's click on **Acquire Data**. This new window will come up:

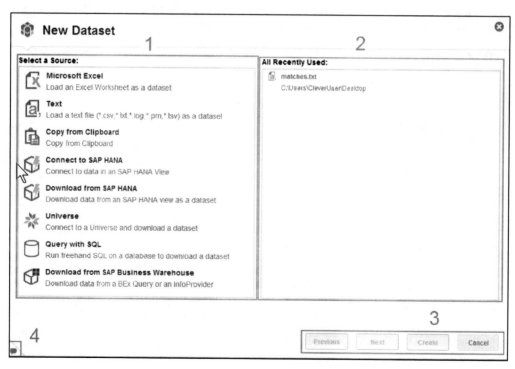

There are areas on this window. They are:

- A list of possible data sources (**1**): Here, the user can connect to his data source.
- Recently used objects (**2**): The user can open his previous connections or files.
- Ordinary buttons (**3**), such as **Previous**, **Next**, **Create**, and **Cancel**.
- This small chat box (**4**) we can find at almost every page. SAP Lumira cares about the quality of the product and gives the opportunity to the user to make a screen print and send feedback to SAP.

Let's go deeper and consider more closely every connection in the table below:

Data Source	Description
Microsoft Excel	Excel data sheets
Flat file	CSV, TXT, LOG, PRN, or TSV
SAP HANA	There are two possible ways: Offline (downloading data) and Online (connected to SAP HANA)
SAP BusinessObjects universe	UNV or UNX
SQL Databases	Query data via SQL from relational databases
SAP Business warehouse	Downloaded data from a BEx Query or an InfoProvider

Let's try to connect some data sources and extract some data from them.

 We will learn about connection to SAP HANA and SAP BusinessObjects universes in *Chapter 7*, *Connecting to SAP BusinessObjects and SAP HANA*.

Microsoft spreadsheets

Let's start with the easiest exercise. For example, our manager of inventory asked us to analyse flop products, which are not popular, and he sent us two excel spreadsheets, Unicorn_flop_products.xls and Unicorn_flop_price.xls. There are two different worksheets because prices and product attributes are in different systems. Both files have a unique field—SKU. As a result, it is possible to merge them by this field and analyse them as one data set.

SKU or stock keeping unit is a distinct item for sale, such as a product or service, and them attributes associated with the item distinguish it from other items. For a product, these attributes include, but are not limited to, manufacturer, product description, material, size, color, packaging, and warranty terms. When a business takes inventory, it counts the quantity of each SKU.

The first task is to acquire the data with SAP Lumira and bind them by SKU number. Let's learn how to handle this challenging task with SAP Lumira:

1. Click **Acquire Data**.
2. Select **Microsoft Excel** source and click **Next**.
3. Find and choose file `Unicorn_flop_products.xls`.
4. A new window pops up— which is a preview of the file.

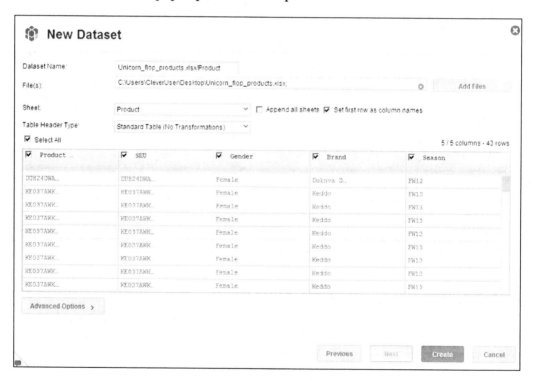

  ○ Notice that we can select a specific sheet from the file, and indicate whether the first row contains column names. In addition, we can also exclude a column from being acquired by clearing the check box on the column header.

○ There are also **Advanced Options** for the dataset:

○ The **Advanced Options** give us a great deal of flexibility in terms of acquiring data from a spreadsheet.

○ Using **Range Selection**, we can choose a subset of rows and/or columns of data. We can specify that our source data is formatted as either a vertical table or a cross table, and SAP Lumira will automatically break down the data appropriately. We can also include or exclude hidden columns or rows, and detect merged cells.

○ In this example, we'll use the default options.

5. After setting the options in the **Preview** window, click **Next,** and the **Prepare** tab will come up:

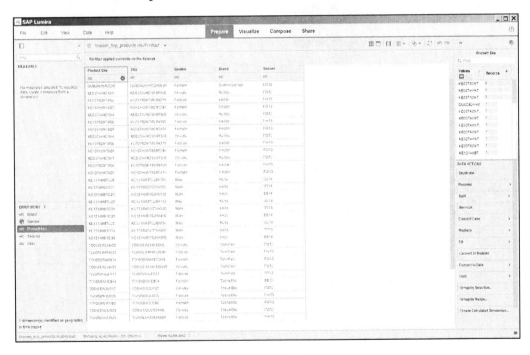

We will miss detailed explanations of this tab in this chapter, because we dive deeper into it in section *Preparing Data* in *Chapter 3, Preparing Data.*

 Tab in Lumira can call rooms.

If you remember, we have a second file and we have to merge it with first one. Let's do it:

1. In the **Prepare** tab, click on **Data->Combine->Merge**:

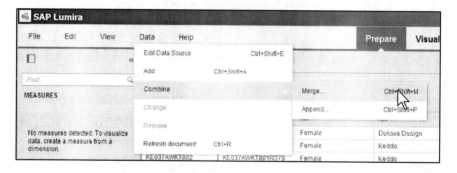

2. A new window appears, **Merge Data**:

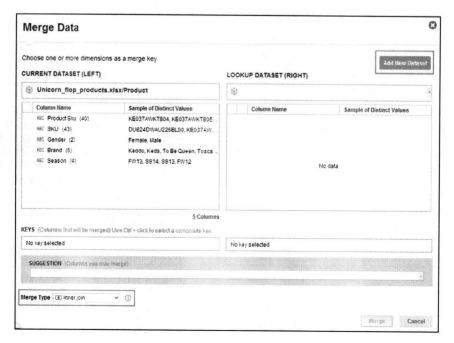

3. In order to add new data, let's click **Add New Dataset**. In addition, there is, **Merge Type** option. For our case, **Inner join** is ok.

Let's review our knowledge of joins:

INNER JOIN: Returns all rows when there is at least one match in *both* tables

LEFT JOIN: Returns all rows from the left table, and the matched rows from the right table

RIGHT JOIN: Returns all rows from the right table, and the matched rows from the left table

FULL JOIN: Returns all rows when there is a match in *one* of the tables

4. Click **Add New Dataset** and choose second file, `Unicorn_flop_prices.xls`. In the following picture you can see the options that were set up automatically.

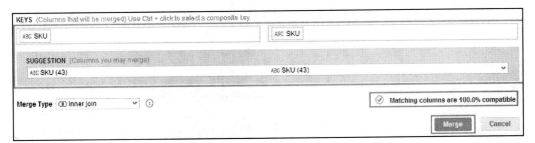

   ° SAP Lumira automatically tries to detect keys for joins. In our example, it is the **SKU** field. In addition, we have the opportunity to replace keys. Moreover, SAP Lumira shows us the percentage of matching columns.

5. Click **Merge** and we will see the **Prepare** tab again, with new column — **Price**.

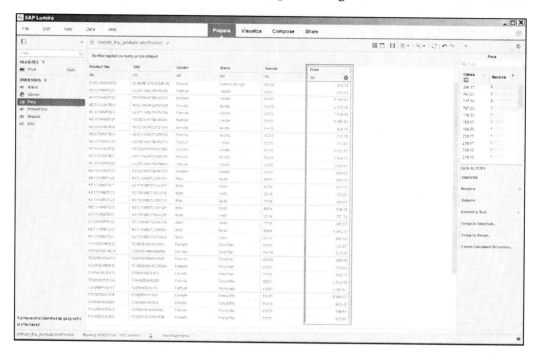

o As a result, we can connect to any Excel file or connect multiple Excel files and connect them together for data analytics.

Text file

Text files are as popular as excel. SAP Lumira can easily work with various structured files, such as CSV, TXT, TSV, and others.

Unicorn Fashion has various delivery methods. In addition, it does its own delivery. It is very important to compare how its own delivery performs versus external companies such as DHL, FedEx, and many more. The operations manager wants information about delivery services. External post services send data about their work, and it is collated together in one CSV file.

Let's try to connect file `Shipping Method Performance.csv`:

1. Click our favorite step—**Acquire Data**.

2. Select a source of **Text**, click **Next**, and choose file `Shipping Method Performance.csv`.

3. This preview window will come up:

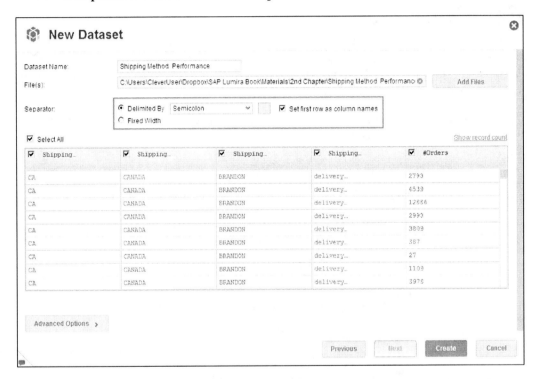

- ° There are not many options in this window. However, we should check that SAP Lumira chooses the right separator. In our example, it is the semicolon. In addition, we can use fixed width instead of a delimiter symbol.

4. Moreover, we can look at **Advanced Options**:

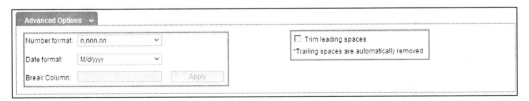

- ° **Advanced Options** allows us to play with the format of numbers and dates, trim leading spaces, and break columns.

5. Then click the **Create** button and that's all; we can play with the data and try to answer the question from the operations manager.

Relational data source

Let's continue to look at the various data connectors for SAP Lumira. One of the most popular are relation data sources. Usually, there are plenty of systems which can provide business insights, such as order systems, warehouse systems, call centre systems, human resources systems, and so on.

Using **Query with SQL** we can create our own data provider by manually entering the SQL for a target data source:

However, users need to be familiar with their database and the SQL language to use **Query with SQL**. You can specify the source tables, columns, and functions to acquire data. In this book we will connect SQL database MySQL via JDBC driver. However, Lumira offers us more options, but they are out of the scope of this book.

SAP Lumira can connect a database via a JDBC driver.

JDBC is a Java database connectivity technology (Java Standard Edition platform) from Oracle Corporation. This technology is an API for the Java programming language that defines how a client may access a database. It provides methods for querying and updating data in a database. JDBC is oriented towards relational databases.

For the complete list of database middleware that can be accessed with **Query with SQL**, refer to the SAP Product Availability Matrix. The following databases, middleware can be connected to by SAP Lumira:

- Amazon EMR Hive
- Apache Derby
- Apache Hadoop Hive
- Cloudera Impala
- Generic JDBC
- Generic ODATA
- Greenplum
- Hewlett Packard NeoView
- IBM DB2
- Netezza
- Ingres Database
- Microsoft SQL Server
- Oracle
- MySQL
- Exadata
- PostgreSQL
- Salesforce
- SAP HANA
- SAP ERP
- SAP R/3
- MySAP ERP
- SAP MII
- MaxDB 7.7
- Sybase
- Teradata

Fortunately, Unicorn Fashion uses MySQL databases and we are able to connect to them via SAP Lumira.

Operational datamart of Unicorn Fashion

For example, in the world of the famous fashion e-commerce retailer Unicorn Fashion there are several transactional systems, which provide operational reporting for business users. In Unicorn Fashion operational means near real time reporting.

In addition, there is a corporate DWH which provides valuable information for supporting business decisions and analysing historical trends. Unicorn Fashion also has available a small operational datamart, which covers two main business processes: Sales and Stocks.

This is a schematic data model of the operational datamart:

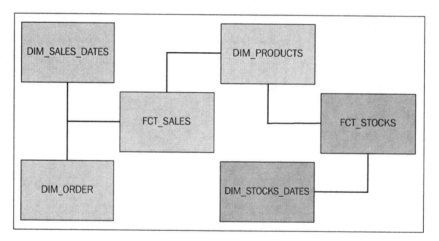

There are several tables in the operational datamart:

- FCT_SALES: This fact table has all the finance data, such as revenue, quantity of items sold, costs, and so on
- DIM_SALES_DATES: The Date attributes of sales data
- DIM_ORDER: Dimensional table, where all shipping and order attributes are based
- DIM_PRODUCTS: Dimensional table for products and articles
- FCT_STOCKS: Fact table which represents the quantity of items in the warehouse
- DIM_STOCKS_DATES: Date attributes of stock date

Setting up the operational datamart

In order to set up the operational datamart we should prepare the database server in order to load data in to it.

Setting up the MySQL database server

Throughout this book, we will see plenty of exercises based on the Unicorn datamart. In order to query the operational datamart, we need to get a copy of this datamart as well as the MySQL database.

 MySQL is the world's most popular open source database. Whether you are a fast growing web property, a technology ISV, or a large enterprise, MySQL can cost-effectively help you deliver high performance, scalable database applications.

Let's download and install MySQL:

1. Go to `http://dev.mysql.com/downloads/installer/`.
2. Choose **mysql-installer-community** and click **Download**.

3. After downloading, run the exe file.
4. Choose setup type **Serve Only** and click **Next**.
5. Click **Execute** and then **Next**.

Let's configure MySQL server:

1. Configure **Type and Networking** as seen in the following screenshot and click **Next**:

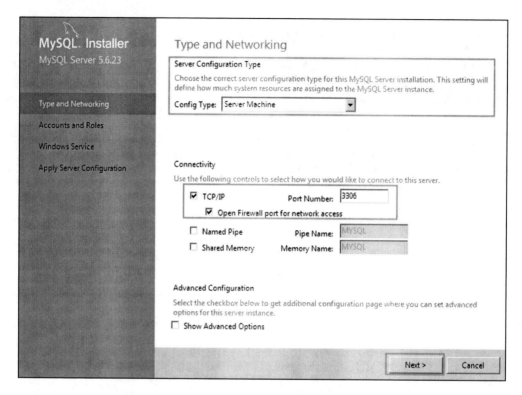

2. Create a root password on tab **Accounts and Roles** and click **Next**.
3. Keep the default **Windows Service**.
4. Select **Apply Server Configuration** and click **Execute**.
5. Finish the installation.

We have successfully installed MySQL database server, and now let's load our data in to it.

Load the Unicorn Fashion datamart

There are scripts for the operational datamart in attachment to this book. There are several SQL files you should download in order to load the datamart:

- `Database_bl.sql`

- `Dim_date.sql`

- `Dim_orders.sql`

- `Dim_products.sql`

- `Fct_sales.sql`

- `Fct_stocks.sql`

As you may guess, we need an SQL Client in order to connect our MySQL server and import the dump files with scripts and data:

1. Let's download and install open source client HeidiSQL from `http://www.heidisql.com/download.php`.

2. Run `HeideSQL.exe` and connect your MySQL Server:

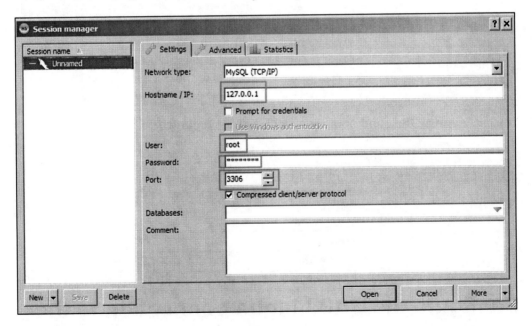

3. We should set the **Hostname** as `localhost` or `127.0.0.1`, **User** as `root`, **Password** as the one created during installation, and `3306` as **Port**. Then click **Open**.

4. The HeidiSQL interface will pop up.

5. We need to create database `BL`. Click **File->Import SQL**.

6. Choose `database_bl.sql` and click **Open**. The script will appear in the script editor:

Dumping database structure for bl

```
CREATE DATABASE IF NOT EXISTS `bl` /*!40100 DEFAULT
CHARACTER SET utf8 */;
USE `bl`;
```

7. Run it and new database `BL` will be created.

8. Import and run all other scripts.

9. Let's check the result:

```
select count(*) from dim_dates;
select count(*) from dim_orders;
select count(*) from dim_products;
select count(*) from fct_sales;
select count(*) from fct_stocks;
```

You can compare the number of rows with the table below:

Table	#Rows
Dim_dates	731
Dim_orders	202155
Dim_products	470253
Fct_sales	479042
FCT_stocks	609800

Configure the SAP Lumira connection to the database

Before starting to query our datamart, we should install the MySQL JDBC driver because, by default, SAP Lumira has a very limited number of drivers.

Let's download and add the JDBC driver for the MySQL database:

1. Download MySQL JDBC driver on `http://dev.mysql.com/downloads/connector/j/`.

2. Extract the driver from the archive.

3. Go to SAP Lumira **File->Preferences->SQL Drivers** and find the MySQL driver:

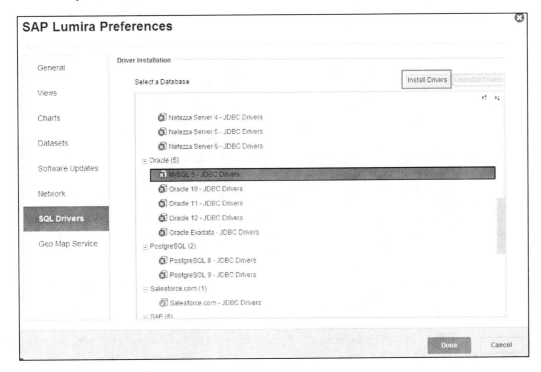

4. Click **Install Drivers** and find **MySQL 5 - JDBC Drivers,** which were downloaded recently. Click **Done**.

5. Restart SAP Lumira.

As a result, SAP Lumira can connect to the MySQL database through the JDBC driver.

Extract data using SQL

The Unicorn Fashion operation datamart is a treasure for analytics because it has all of the valuable information which is important for operational reporting and supporting the business decision process.

Let's try to query the Unicorn Fashion datamart BL:

 BL is shorthand for Business Layer.

1. Click on **Acquire Data**.
2. Choose **Query with SQL** and click **Next**.
3. Select **MySQL JDBC** and click **Next**.
4. Enter your login credentials to continue, including the **Server** and port number as in the following screenshot, and click **Connect**:

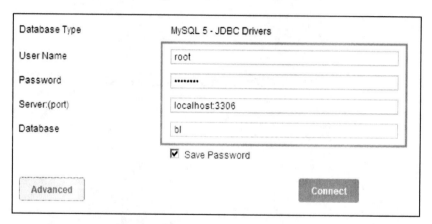

These are the same credentials as used in HeidiSQL. In addition, you can click **Advanced**, where you can find complex database parameters. Keep it as the default.

5. Paste the SQL query below in to the **Query** tab:

```
SELECT
    dim_orders.Shipping_City_Name,
    dim_products.Category,
    sum(fct_sales.Revenue),
    sum(fct_sales.Shipped_Item)
FROM
```

```
dim_orders INNER JOIN fct_sales ON (dim_orders.Order_Id=fct_
sales.Order_Id)
   INNER JOIN dim_products ON (dim_products.Article_Id=fct_sales.
Article_Id)
   INNER JOIN dim_dates  Sales_Dates ON (Sales_Dates.Date_Nat_
Id=fct_sales.Order_Date_Nat_Id)

WHERE
   Sales_Dates.Iso_Date  BETWEEN   {d '2012-01-01 00:00:00'}   AND
{d '2012-01-05 00:00:00'}
GROUP BY
   dim_orders.Shipping_City_Name,
   dim_products.Category
```

6. It is possible to see a preview. Then click **Create** and a new dataset will be created. This data shows us how much money Unicorn Fashion has earned by **Category** and **City** between January and January 05.

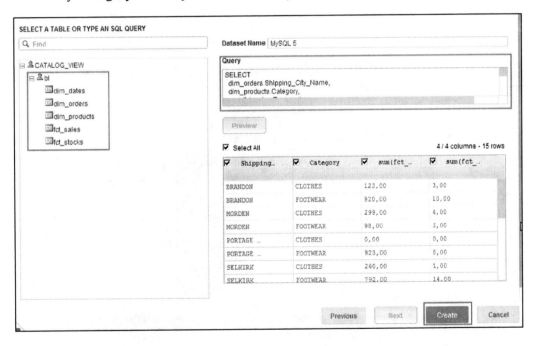

Save the dataset as `Revenue by City and Category`.

Manage connections and associated documents

From the sidebar, we can access the **Connections** page, which we can use to view and edit all the connections defined between documents and data sources.

The **Connections** pane lists all of the data sources that are used by our SAP Lumira documents. If we have a long list of datasets, we can use the search feature to find specific datasets by name:

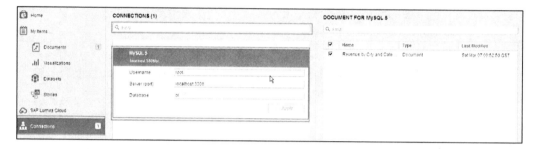

It is possible to change the credentials of the data source. As a result, all documents will replace their data source automatically.

Big data source

It is not a secret that technologies such as Apache Hadoop are very popular with organizations because it is scalable, cheap, and relatively easy to get data into Hadoop. There are plenty of tools for getting data into different formats, and there are some tools that give us the opportunity to get data from Hadoop via SQL, such as Apache Hive or Cloudera Impala.

> Apache Hadoop is an open source software project that enables distributed storing and processing of large data sets across clusters of commodity servers.
>
> Apache Hive is a data warehouse infrastructure built on top of Apache Hadoop for providing data summarization, query, and analysis.
> Cloudera Impala is Cloudera's open source **Massively Parallel Processing (MPP)** SQL query engine for data stored in a computer cluster running Apache Hadoop.

SAP Lumira is a modern data discovery tool which is designed to work with big data. It is pretty much the same to query Hadoop via SQL with Hive or Impala. And you can try to do it following the instructions of this video: http://scn.sap.com/docs/DOC-61453 — Connect to Hortonworks Sandbox.

SAP applications

Very often SAP Lumira complements SAP applications and products, such as SAP BusinessObjects and SAP HANA.

SAP BusinessObjects BI (also known as BO or BOBI) is a suite of front-end applications that allow business users to view, sort, and analyze business intelligence data.

SAP HANA is an in-memory, column-oriented, relational database management system developed and marketed by SAP SE. HANA's architecture is designed to handle both high transaction rates and complex query processing on the same platform. SAP HANA was previously called SAP High-Performance Analytic Appliance.

It is very important to know how to connect SAP Lumira to SAP BusinessObjects universes, or SAP HANA data, because it is one of core purpose of SAP Lumira to compliment and extend these products.

We will go deeper in to the integration process between SAP Lumira and SAP applications and products in *Chapter 7, Connecting to SAP BusinessObjects BI Platform and SAP HANA*.

Summary

In this chapter we have learned how SAP Lumira can acquire various types of data from various data sources, such as text files, Microsoft Excel spreadsheets, databases, and so on. There are plenty of options which can help us to configure our connection. In addition, we set up MySQL server and loaded the Unicorn Fashion datamart, which will provide data for the following chapters and exercises.

In the next chapter, we will learn about preparing data and what SAP Lumira offer us in order to make our data valuable and useful.

3
Preparing Data

Data is everywhere, and it has various formats and types. Sometimes it is structured, whereas sometimes it is not. Data discovery is a challenging process because, in most cases, we should work with massive volumes of raw data in order to find business insights. Business or data analysts have to work hard in order to prepare data and understand data patterns, highlight unique values, or just format and clean the data.

Once all this data has been collected, the data geek must prepare the data that has to be analyzed. Organizing the data correctly can save a lot of time and prevent mistakes. With SAP Lumira, they can format data to fit their needs in order to organize their data effectively. A good data geek enters all the data in the same format and in the same place because doing otherwise may lead to confusion and difficulty with statistical analysis later on. Once the data has been entered, it is crucial that the data geek checks the data for accuracy. This can be accomplished by spot-checking a random assortment of participant data groups, but this method is not as effective as re-entering the data a second time and searching for discrepancies. This method is particularly easy to perform when you use numerical data because the analyst can simply use SAP Lumira to sum the columns of the spreadsheet and then look for differences in the totals.

In this chapter, we will cover the following topics:

- Preparing view
- Cleaning data
- Filtering and formatting data
- Enriching data
- Merging data

Preparing a data tab

In the previous chapter, you learned how to extract data from various data sources. When we connected to data, we got a new window, called the **Prepare** tab, with our data in it. It has many features to clean, filter, and merge data. Let's look closely at the **Prepare** tab and the main bars. But, before this, we need to extract and acquire some data. Perform the following steps:

1. First, click on **Acquire Data**.

2. Then select **Query with SQL**.

3. Next, select the recently used connection that we created in the previous chapter; it offers us the opportunity to use our SQL query.

4. Then click on **Preview** and **Create**.

5. The **Prepare** tab will appear:

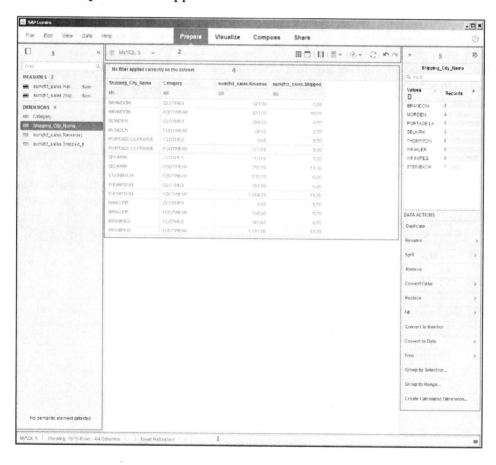

6. There are five main tabs on the **Prepare** window

   ○ The status bar (1): This is visible in all workspaces and displays details about the dataset, such as the name, the number of rows and columns, and the last refreshed date and time. We can also submit feedback about SAP Lumira from here to SAP.

   ○ The prepare workspace (2): This is where you edit and clean the data from your datasets. The toolbar for the **Prepare** workspace provides access to common commands, such as toggling between datasets in a document, switching between *Grid* and *Facet* modes, showing and hiding columns, creating calculated dimensions and measures, merging and appending records, refreshing values, undoing or redoing steps, and deleting or creating datasets. Here is the table with the details about *Grid* and *Facets* modes:

Visualizing data as	Description
Grid	This specifies that the data is presented as columns and rows. All the rows are displayed here.
Facets	This denotes that the data is presented as columns with only the unique values shown. The repeated values in these columns are not shown. Here, using facets can be useful if you have many repeated values.

   ○ The object picker pane (3): This organizes the different types of data available in our datasets into measures, dimensions, and so on. If necessary, we can search for specific items by name. There are four types of object:

Object Picker objects	Description
Measure	This maps to aggregated data in a column or calculation. You can use **Measures** to get the calculated result when different columns are combined. For example, a measure called **Sales Revenue** would represent the **Sales Revenue** column that contains the total revenue for sales. Measures are automatically detected and listed.

Hierarchies	This references more than one related column in your dataset. These columns have hierarchical relationships; for example, an object **Time** could include **Year**, **Quarter**, and **Month** arranged in a hierarchical structure under the top object of **Time**.
Attributes	This maps to columns in the dataset.
Inferred dimensions	This maps one or more columns that are created based on the geography or time data available to SAP Lumira in order to support a hierarchy. For example, if you select **Create a geographic hierarchy** for the dimension **City**, you can select the levels of the hierarchy (**Country**, **Region**, and **City**). SAP Lumira infers the **Country** and **Region** from a geography database, and the **Country** and **Region** columns are created that match the **City** values. These columns are added to the dataset, but are not part of the original dataset. They are inferred and added to support the hierarchy.

°   Each dimension and measure in the object picker pane also has a menu of additional commands, as shown in the following screenshot:

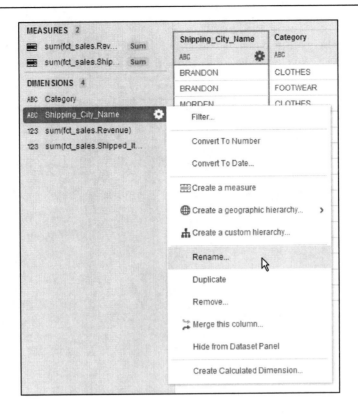

- ○ The values (**4**) from the dataset are displayed in the main window, in either the grid or facet format, using icons in the column or facet headers to indicate the data type: **ABC** for strings, **123** for numbers, a calendar for dates, a globe for geographical hierarchies, and a clock for time hierarchies.

There are also menus in each column, or facet headers, that let us perform additional commands for each measure or dimension.

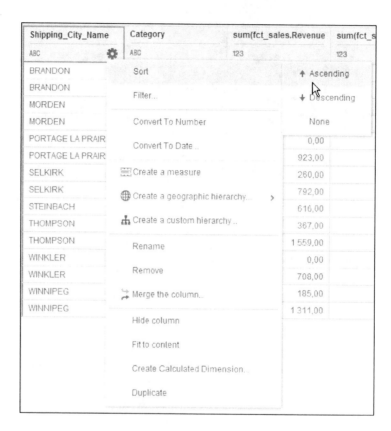

- The sidebar (5) contains tools that we can use to manipulate the data in any selected column, such as replacing values, changing case, trimming leading and trailing spaces.

Now that you have learned about the main features of the **Preview** tab, let's play with the data for Unicorn Fashion.

Preparing data

Usually, there is raw data in the data source and we want to analyse it from another view. However, sometimes it is not formatted consistently. As a result, it is not easily interpreted by business users. Before creating reports and visualizations, it is often necessary to clean up the data so that it is presentable and understandable.

Cleaning and editing a dataset

Say we want to exclude **Shipping City** from our dataset in order to analyse the revenue and quantity of items by category. In addition, we want to reduce the dataset and improve performance. This can be done easily with the following steps:

1. Click on **Data->Edit Data Source** or press *Ctrl+Shift+E*; the **Edit Data Source** window will appear:

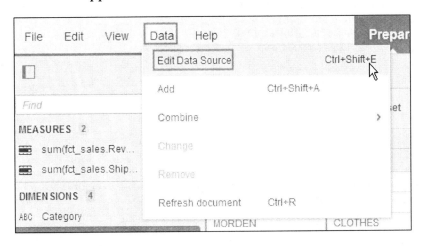

2. Uncheck **Shipping City** and click on **OK**.

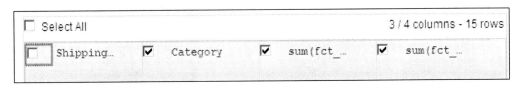

We will get the new dataset with only three columns.

Let's continue to learn how to prepare our data on another SQL query that returns much more data. Perform the following steps:

1. Click on **File->New**. Select **Query with SQL**.

2. From the **Recently Used** tab, select our MySQL connection and click on **Connect**.

3. The **New Dataset** window will open.

4. Enter the new SQL query:

```
SELECT
CONCAT(dim_products.Category,':',dim_products.`Sub-category`) as
Category,
dim_products.Product_Name,
dim_products.Brand,
dim_orders.Shipping_City_Name,
dim_orders.Shipping_Method,
fct_sales.Discount_Percent,
DATE_FORMAT(Sales_Dates.Iso_Date,'%d/%m/%y') as Sales_Date,
sum(fct_sales.Revenue)
FROM
dim_orders INNER JOIN fct_sales ON (dim_orders.Order_Id=fct_sales.
Order_Id)
INNER JOIN dim_products ON (dim_products.Article_Id=fct_sales.
Article_Id)
INNER JOIN dim_dates  Sales_Dates ON (Sales_Dates.Date_Nat_Id=fct_
sales.Order_Date_Nat_Id)
WHERE
Sales_Dates.Iso_Date  BETWEEN  {d '2012-01-01 00:00:00'}  AND  {d
'2012-02-29 00:00:00'}
GROUP BY
dim_products.Category,
dim_products.`Sub-category`,
dim_products.Product_Name,
dim_products.Brand,
dim_orders.Shipping_City_Name,
dim_orders.Shipping_Method,
fct_sales.Discount_Percent,
Sales_Date
```

The preceding SQL query returns the answerset for the period, giving revenue for various products across cities by shipping methods.

Enter the new name of the dataset, `Product Analytics`, and then click on **Preview** and **Create**.

5. We have successfully created the new dataset: **Product Analytics**.

There are some issues with the data that we have to fix before we visualize our data. We should be able to edit the metadata and the content of the dataset without changing the original datasource.

Formatting dates

Our SQL script returned data in the following date format: dd/mm/yy, which is in the string format, as shown in the following screenshot:

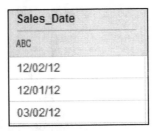

This type of data is not so comfortable for analyzing purposes. Let's change the data type to date and the format to dd.mm.yyyy with the following steps:

1. Click on the column header. In the sidebar, click on **Convert to Date**, select **dd/MM/yy** as the appropriate type, and click on **Apply**:

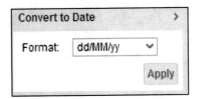

2. We can see that a new column called **Sales_Date(2)** has been added to the dataset to store the converted values. The original column is still available:

Sales_Date	Sales_Date (2)
ABC	🗓14 ⚙
05/02/12	05.02.2012
05/02/12	05.02.2012
29/01/12	29.01.2012
03/02/12	03.02.2012

Additional, we can rename **Sales Date (2)** and hide **Sales Date**.

The split field

Let's take a look at the **Category** field. We can see that the **Category** column includes both the **Category** and **Sub-Category** information, separated by a colon:

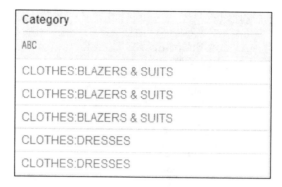

We can use the manipulation tools to create individual **Category** and **Sub-Category** columns by splitting the existing column. Let's split the field with the following steps:

1. First, click on the **Category** header. In the sidebar, click on **Split** and select **<Colon>**:

2. Then, click on **Apply**.

3. Two new dimensions called **Category (2)** and **Category (3)** are created. These contain the split data. Now, let's rename these two new dimensions as follows:

Category	Category (2)	Category (3)
ABC	ABC	ABC
CLOTHES:JEANS	CLOTHES	JEANS
CLOTHES:JEANS	CLOTHES	JEANS
CLOTHES:JEANS	CLOTHES	JEANS

Renaming a column

We can access common commands, such as renaming, from the menu for the individual columns. Let's rename two new columns using the following steps:

1. First, click on the column header of **Category (2)**.

2. Then click on the column menu and select **Rename**:

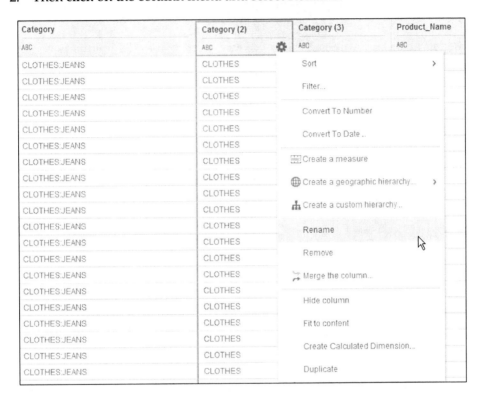

3. Rename **Category (2)** as **Main Category** and **Category (1)** as **Sub-Category**, as shown in the following screenshot:

Main Category	Sub-Category
ABC	ABC
CLOTHES	BLAZERS & SUITS
CLOTHES	BLAZERS & SUITS
CLOTHES	BLAZERS & SUITS
CLOTHES	DRESSES
CLOTHES	DRESSES

Distinct values

In addition to the grid format, in which we worked before, we can also display measures and dimensions in the facet format, which shows the unique values for each unique field, making it easier for us to clean our data. Now, let's click on facets:

We will get the unique values for each column, as shown in the following screenshot:

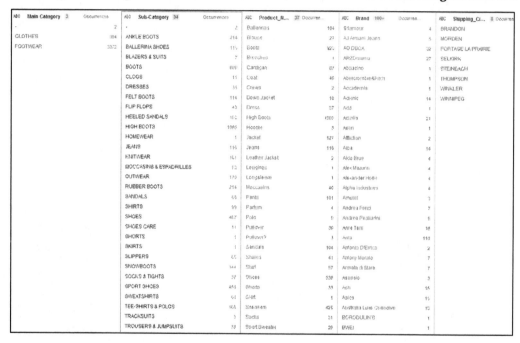

In facets mode, we can easily overview and identify the issues with the data.

Replacing data values

Here we can see that values are missing in the **Main Category** and **Sub-Category** columns:

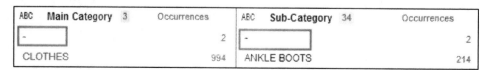

Let's fix this issue with the following steps:

1. Click on the **Main Category** header. In the sidebar, click on **Replace**:

Enter `Technical` in the **Replace** section.

2. Then click on **Apply,** and repeat this for **Sub-Category**.

Connection between values

In the facets view, you can also right-click on any value to highlight the related values and dimensions. In other words, it is a kind of hierarchy where you can choose any value and look at the related values from other fields, as shown in the following screenshot:

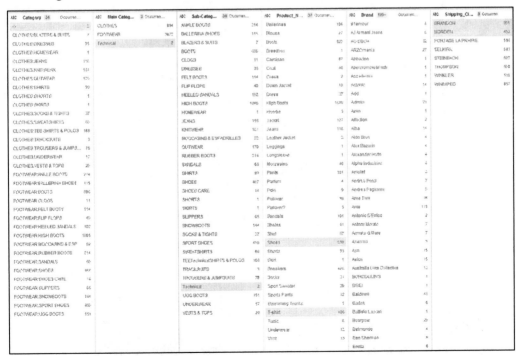

We are ready to clean our dataset. Let's enrich it.

Enriching data

SAP Lumira offers you various methods to enrich your dataset by adding measures, geography hierarchies, and time hierarchies. **Measures** allow you to easily manipulate calculations, and hierarchies allow you to use a natural grouping of related columns.

SAP Lumira detects columns that are potential measures, time hierarchies, and geography hierarchies when we acquire data.

The time hierarchy

By default, we have only **Sales Date**, but for a detailed historical analysis, we need to analyze various date dimensions, such as year, month, week, and so on.

Let's create the time hierarchy for **Sales Date** with the following steps:

1. Click on the option menu for the **Sales Date** dimension:

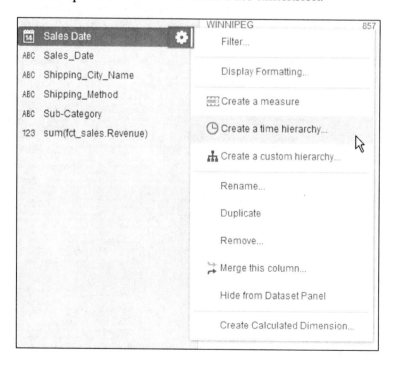

2. Then select **Create a time hierarchy....**
3. SAP Lumira will create new date dimensions as follows:

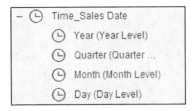

The geographical hierarchy

Modern analytics tools provide us with the opportunity to look at data from the geographical perspective. It gives us lots of advantages: for example, we can easily measure the region that is the most popular with customers and the product that is the most popular in a particular city or region.

 Geography hierarchies can only be created on columns that contain values that are compatible with geographic data values in the NAVTEQ database used by SAP Lumira.

Unicorn Fashion is operating in Manitoba, Canada. The category manager wants to know the performance of various subcategories in different cities.

Unfortunately, there is no longitude or latitude data in the operational datamart. However, we can find the longitude and latitude of cities and map them with cities in the datamart.

Let's learn how to merge the new dataset with the existing dataset in order to create a geographical hierarchy. Perform the following steps:

1. First, let's click on **Data->Combine->Merge**:

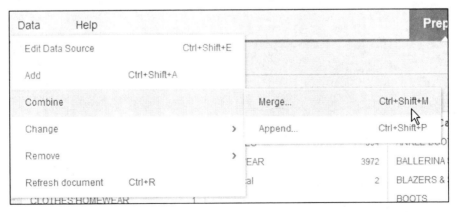

A new window will appear. Here we have to select the new data source.

We can combine the data from two different datasets using JOIN.

The dataset columns for the second dataset are matched based on its compatibility with a key column. The matched columns are proposed using the probability of the match. The following conditions are required before two datasets can be merged:

- The merging dataset must have a key column
- Only columns with the same data type are considered
- The merged dataset adds all the columns

We can append two datasets with a UNION operator only when each table in the union contains an equivalent number of columns with compatible data types. Only a selected dataset that is union-compatible with the target dataset will be displayed in the merge databox.

2. Now click on **Add New Dataset** and select **Text file**. Then select the Geo map.csv file with **City, latitude**, and **longitude**. SAP Lumira will automatically join both the datasets using the city name:

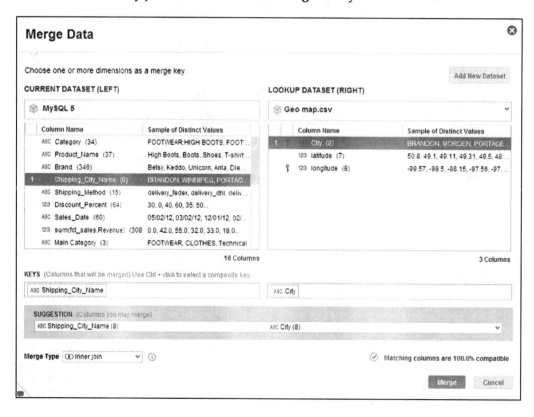

When you click on **Merge**, new fields will be added to the existing dataset as follows:

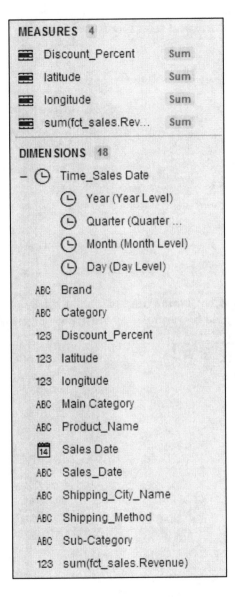

SAP Lumira will automatically create measures based on latitude and longitude. Unfortunately, SAP Lumira can automatically recognize numeric values as measures. Let's delete both of the measures by clicking on the properties of measure and selecting **Remove**:

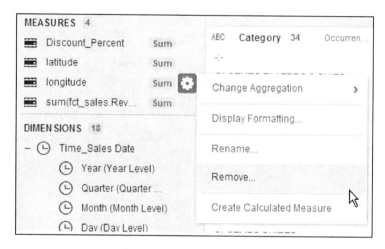

3. In the **Shipping_City_Name** dimension list, click on options and select **Create a geographic hierarchy->By Latitude/Longitude**:

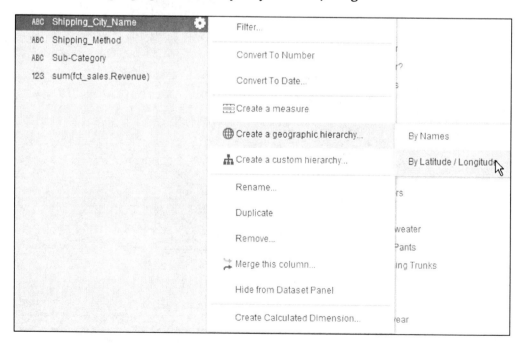

4. The **Geographical data** window will appear. Enter the **Latitude** and **Longitude** and select **City** as **Geographical level**:

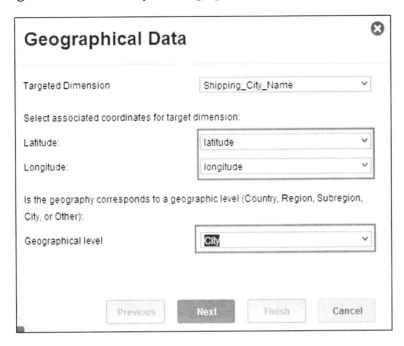

5. Then click on **Next**. Select the geographical parents level, such as **Country**, **Region**, and **Sub-Region**. Click on **Finish**.

The new hierarchy will appear:

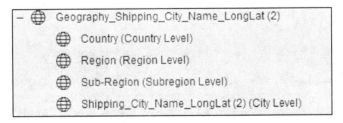

Additional, we can adjust this a little bit and rename some dimensions.

The custom hierarchy

SAP Lumira also offers us the opportunity to build a custom hierarchy of dimensions, such as **Category**, **Sub-Category**, and **Brand**. As a result, we can drill down the report. In order to create a custom hierarchy, we need to select **Create a custom hierarchy** from the **Dimensions** menu:

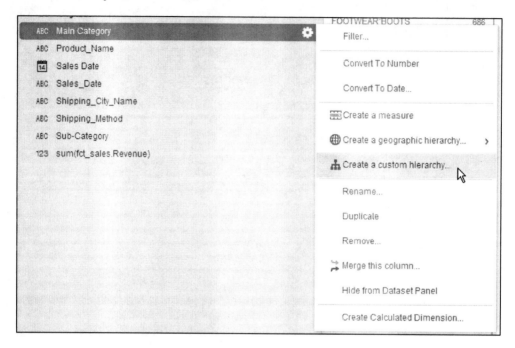

Then add all of the **Dimensions** in descending order.

Creating the calculated object

Finally, we will create new calculated measures or dimensions in our dataset using formulas that are based on the existing measures. In this example, we'll create a calculated measure for revenue based on the prognosis of sales analytics that the revenue in the next month will be 10 percent less than in both previous months together.

Perform the following steps:

1. Click on the options menu for measure and select **Create Calculated Measure**.

2. The **New Calculated Measure** window will appear.

3. Enter the new formula in the formula editor:

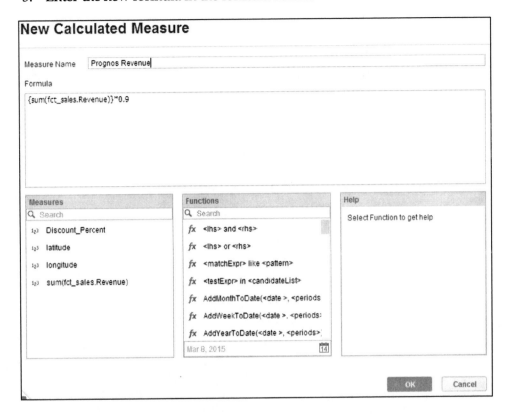

SAP Lumira provides us with many functions that can help us calculate complex measures. You can learn more about these functions in the functions tab by choosing any function from the list in order to get detailed help about this function.

In addition, we can create new dimensions in the same way.

Summary

In this chapter, you have learned how to prepare data and why it is very important to clean data before starting to analyze it in detail. You have also looked at the rich functionalities that SAP Lumira offers to prepare and enrich data. We have discussed several techniques, such as merging and appending datasets, splitting column values, creating various hierarchies, creating new objects, and so on. These techniques will help you to prepare and produce better visualizations in the next chapter.

4
Visualizing Data and Telling Stories with It

"The shortest distance between truth and a human being is a story."

Anthony de Mello, One Minute Wisdom

In the previous chapters, you learned how to connect and prepare data for data discovery purposes. This chapter is a core chapter because you will learn what we can actually do with our data. In order to find our data business insights in vast amounts of data, we should slice and dice our data. It is not a secret that vision is our dominant sense. As a result, it is much easier to find answers to a business question in a massive pile of data when you visualize it.

SAP Lumira offers us a rich set of chart types. This can help to make our raw data more sensible and useful, which will help us to understand trends, find outages, and make better decisions faster. In addition, we can tell a story based on our data. This gives us advantages and helps other people figure out what the data actually wants to tell us.

In this chapter, we will cover the following topics:

- Various data visualization techniques of SAP Lumira
- How to tell stories based on our data
- How to create attractive infographic

The visualization data tab

After preparing data, we can start to work with it more closely. In other words, we can visualize it with the charts in SAP Lumira.

Let's take a look at the visualization tab, and try various options and menus in order to build sharp visualizations like a data geek. Perform the following steps:

1. Click on **File->New**.

2. Select **Query with SQL** and our recently used connection from the MySQL database.

3. Enter the dataset name as `Business Analytics` and paste this SQL query:

```
SELECT
    dim_products.Category,
    dim_products.`Sub-category`,
    dim_products.Brand,
    dim_products.Gender,
    dim_orders.Shipping_City_Name,
    dim_orders.Shipping_Method,
    fct_sales.Order_Date,
    dim_products.Price,
    sum(fct_sales.Revenue),
    sum(fct_sales.Shipped_Item),
    sum(dim_orders.Order_Shipped)
FROM
    dim_orders INNER JOIN fct_sales ON (dim_orders.Order_Id=fct_
sales.Order_Id)
    INNER JOIN dim_products ON (dim_products.Article_Id=fct_sales.
Article_Id)

GROUP BY
    dim_products.Category,
    dim_products.`Sub-category`,
    dim_products.Brand,
    dim_products.Gender,
    dim_orders.Shipping_City_Name,
    dim_orders.Shipping_Method,
    fct_sales.Order_Date,
    dim_products.Price
```

The preceding query returns information about each product, its revenue, and its shipping cost across shipping cities.

4. Click on **Create**. The **Visualize** tab will appear:

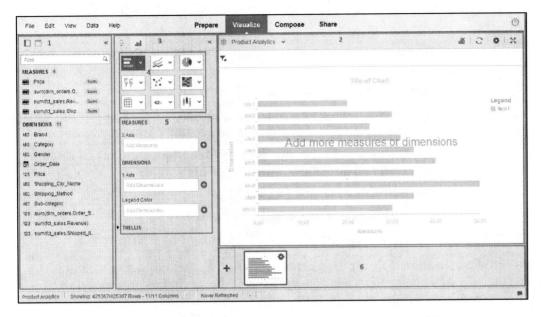

Let's take a closer look at the menu of the visualize tab:

- The **Measures** and **Dimensions** panel (**1**): This panel can be used to view, sort, select, and filter the data in visualization. The data in the panel is grouped into facets, which represent categories of data. For example, customer name, address, and phone number. Facets can be dragged directly to the chart canvas or shelves in the chart builder. The two orientation icons provide different functionalities:

    ○ In the vertical layout, you can view and expand the dimension hierarchies. You can search for dimensions by name.

    ○ In the horizontal layout, the data associated with each dimension is displayed in a column before the chart area. You can search for specific data values within a dimension. You can also select multiple values to include or exclude it from your visualization and view the measures associated with a dimension.

- The chart canvas (**2**): This area can be used to create, modify, or explore a visualization. A chart can be built by dragging measures, dimensions, or facet headers either:

    ○ Directly onto the chart canvas

    ○ Onto the shelves in the chart builder

You can quickly adjust the content and appearance of your visualization using the toolbar in the upper-right corner of the chart canvas. The toolbar contains the following buttons:

- **Reprompt**: This opens the prompt dialog box so that you can select new prompt values

- **Sort**: This organizes the chart data by measure

- **Add or edit a ranking by measure**: This makes the chart focus on a certain number of the highest or lowest dimension members

- **The clear chart**: This removes all the dimensions and measures from the chart, and any filters applied only to the chart

- **Refresh**: This refreshes the chart data

- **Settings**: This sets the properties of the chart

- **Maximize**: This expands the chart canvas to fullscreen mode

- Visualization tools (**3**): This panel contains the chart builder tab and the related visualizations tab. Use the icons at the top of this area to switch between the tabs:

  - Use the chart builder tab to change the chart type and customize your chart.

  - Use the related visualizations tab to select the predefined charts that have been automatically generated based on the measures and dimensions in the current dataset. Related visualizations can be added to the current story and modified. Use this tab to also access influence analysis, which suggests visualizations based on how dimensions contribute to a selected measure.

- The chart picker (**4**): This selects the type of chart we want to use for the visualization.

- Shelves (**5**): Facets can be dragged or added onto the shelves that appear, and the chart canvas will be automatically updated.

- The visualization gallery (**6**): This area can be used to create new visualizations and select between visualizations in the story. We can create a new visualization by clicking on the **Create new visualization** button. We can use the **Settings** menu to remove or duplicate visualizations. We can also change the order of the visualizations in the visualization gallery by dragging and dropping them.

Building visualization

Now that we have successfully loaded data into SAP Lumira from the MySQL database and have several dimensions and measures, let's create some charts and try the various options of SAP Lumira. However, before we start, we should create a geographical hierarchy like we did in the previous chapter, where we added the Excel spreadsheet with the latitude, longitude, and rename fields.

Visualizations are limited to 30,000 data points with interactivity and 100,000 data points with no interactivity due to screen size limitations and its ability to visualize larger amounts of data. A warning appears when this limit is exceeded, and you are asked to filter the set.

In the latest release of SAP Lumira, you can also view the data using the HTML5 technology. There are certain limitations in HTML5 mode that are specific to this release, including a limit of 3,000 data points for visualizations. This will be addressed in the following releases.

Renaming fields

Before we start, let's rename fields in a normal way. Perform the following steps:

Click on the **Measures** option and select **Rename**:

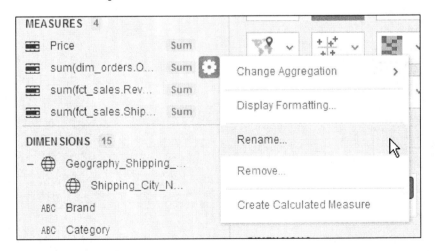

We rename **dim_orders.order_shipped** as **Shipped Orders**, **fct_sales.revenue** as **Revenue**, and **fct_sales.shipped_item** as **Shipped Items**. In addition, we should replace _ with blank from other fields.

In *Chapter 3, Preparing Data*, we looked at how to rename fields and complete other operations with data on the **Prepare** tab.

We can drag and drop or use the **Add** button from the chart feeder to add measures and dimensions to the chart.

Creating the column chart

Let's create a report in order to find the top 10 brands for Unicorn Fashion with the following steps:

1. First, select **Column Chart**.

2. Then select **Revenue** as **Y Axis**, **Brand** as **X Axis**:

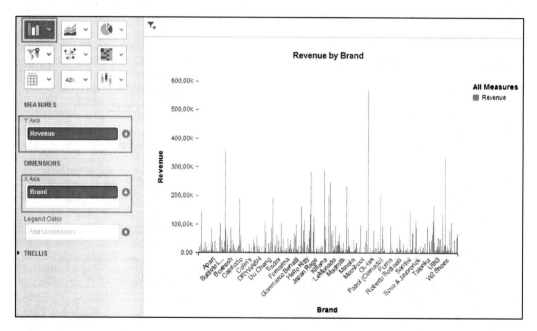

The sort order

Let's sort our brands by **Revenue**. Perform the following steps:

Click on the list for **Revenue** and select **Sort Descending**:

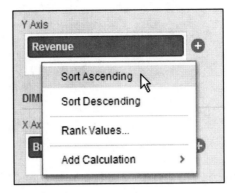

As a result, SAP Lumira sorted various brands by revenue.

Ranking dimensions

In order to find the top 10 brands, we should apply the rank option to our chart. Let's select the top 10 brands that give us the most revenue. Perform the following steps:

1. Click on the list for **Revenue** and select **Rank Values**:

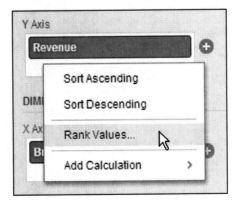

2. The **Ranking** window will appear. Enter **10** and select **Brand**:

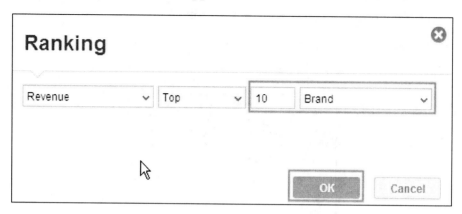

3. Click on **OK**. As a result, there are only top 10 brands left.

4. Rename the chart as `Top 10 Brands by Revenue`, select **Show Gridlines** and hide legend because it is useless fro this chart:

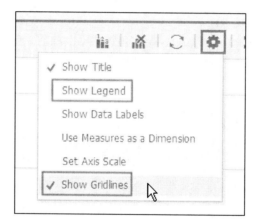

As a result, we should get this chart:

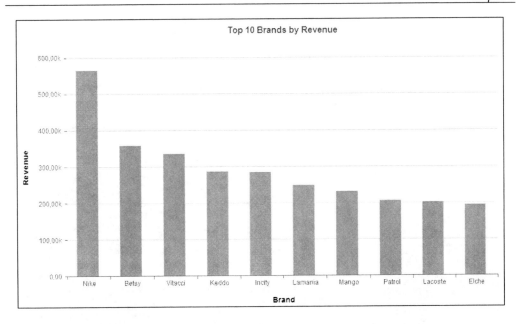

Creating the geographic chart

SAP Lumira offers various options for geo visualizations when we want to show a map of the country object used in the analysis. We may also need to see the data for dimensions, sorted by country, shown on the map, or we may want to see the geographical spread of data for any single country. There are four types of charts:

- The Geo Bubble chart
- The Geo Choropleth chart
- The Geo Pie chart
- The Geo Map

Our dataset must contain the geographical dimension, shipping city, based on longitude and latitude. By default, Lumira has weak geo visualizations, but it offers us the opportunity to use external plugins, such as ArcGis. Perform the following steps:

1. Navigate to the Esri website and create an account at `http://www.esri.com/software/arcgis/arcgisonline`:

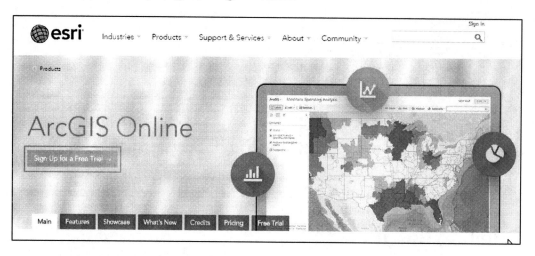

2. Then sign up for the free trial.
3. Navigate to SAP Lumira preferences.
4. Select **Geo Map Services** and enter your credentials for ArcGis.

As a result, we can use the ArcGis map for geo visualization. Let's build the report in order to understand how various shipping methods perform in operating cities through the following steps:

1. First, click on **Create New Data Visualization**.
2. Then select **Geo Map** from **Geographical charts**.
3. Next select bubble as **Data Point Type**.
4. Then select **Shipping City Name** as **Geo Dimension**, **Shipped Orders** as **Size**, and **Shipping Method** as **Color**:

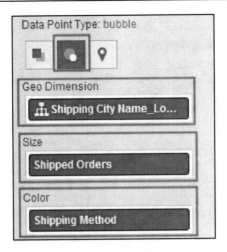

Filter dimensions

Sometimes we need to exclude the wrong values or inaccurate data. Let's exclude the bad shipping method: **No Value**. Perform the following steps:

1. Click on **Add Filter** and select **Shipping method**:

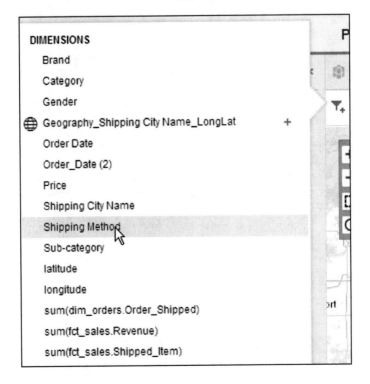

2. Then exclude **null**:

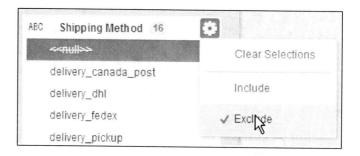

3. As a result, we will get a very nice map chart:

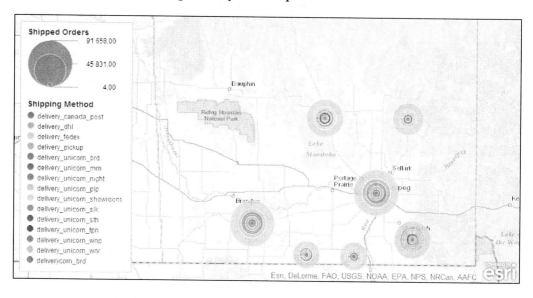

Unfortunately for Unicorn Fashion, most orders were shipped by an external delivery service: Fedex. Unicorn constantly develops its own delivery method and wants to decrease the number of shipping orders by external logistics companies. As a result, it is very important for the operation manager to keep an eye on these metrics.

Creating the area chart

Let's try to understand the trends for shipping methods.

Creating the calculated dimension

In order to compare performance between the internal and external deliveries, we can create a new field called **Shipping Method Type**. Perform the following steps:

1. Let's click on the list for **Shipping Method** and select **Creating Calculated Dimension**.

2. Then create a new dimension called **Shipping Method Type**:

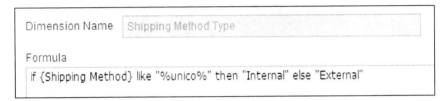

Enter the preceding code or invent a new one.

3. Then click on **OK**.

Let's continue to create the area chart with the following steps:

1. Select **Area Chart** in **Visualization Tools**.

2. Drag and drop **Shipped Orders** to **Y Axis**, **Order Date** to **X Axis**, and **Shipping Method Type** to **Legend Color**.

3. In chart properties, select **100%** stacking.

4. Rename the data visualization as **Shipped Orders by Shipping Type**:

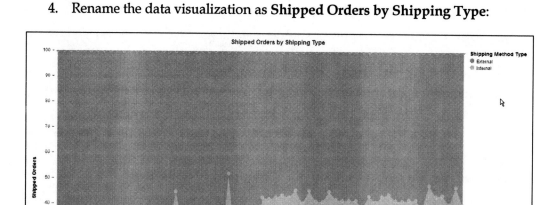

As a result, we can see that our own delivery services account for almost 50 percent of orders and is one of the primary KPIs of a successful e-commerce company.

Creating multiple charts

Sometimes we want to compare the same metrics via multiple charts based on a particular dimension. Let's learn how to do this via SAP Lumira. Let's create the visualization to show the category groups in different charts, rather than as unique colors. In addition, we have a subcategory and brand. Based on our experience, we want to create a custom hierarchy with the option of drill-down to subcategory and brand.

Creating a custom hierarchy

In the previous chapter, you learned about custom hierarchies. Now, let's create one with the following steps:

1. Select **Create Custom Hierarchy** for the **Category** dimension.

2. Enter the name as Category Hierarchy.

3. Add the **Sub-Category** and **Brand** children under **Category**.

4. Click on **OK**.

As a result, we will get a new custom hierarchy with the default name as **Hierarchy**:

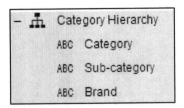

Creating trellis

We can create a trellis effect to divide our visualization into multiple charts for each member in a particular dimension. Let's try this. Perform the following steps:

1. Select **Column Chart** in visualization tools.

2. Drag and drop **Revenue** to **Y Axis** and select **Shipping Method** as **Legend Color**. **X Axis** will remain blank.

3. Select **Category** as **Columns** in the TRELLIS menu:

4. Filter **Category** so that you have **FOOTWEAR** and **CLOTHES**.

As a result, we will get multiple charts:

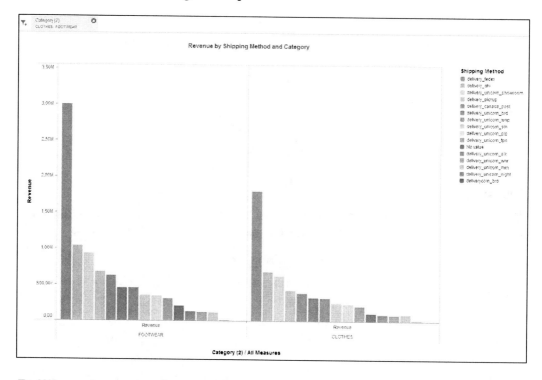

Drilling down and up

SAP Lumira allows you to drill down if the dimension that contains a hierarchy is included in a chart. We can drill down through the data available on the chart canvas, one level at a time.

In order to drill down, we need to click on the value of the dimension with hierarchy: for example, **FOOTWEAR**:

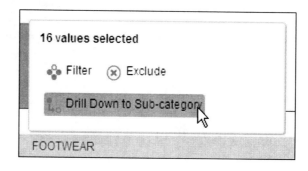

Select **Drill Down to Sub-category**. On the other hand, we can drill up by clicking on **Drill Up to Level Up**.

Creating out-of-the-box charts

SAP Lumira allows you to use various interesting charts, such as the **Funnel Chart**, **Tag Cloud**, the **Radar Chart**, and so on. Let's take a look at some of them.

Creating a tag cloud

Nowadays, it is very popular to create a tag cloud, especially for blogs or other media. Let's try to create one. Perform the following steps:

1. Select **Tag Cloud** in visualization tools.

 A tag cloud, a word cloud, or a weighted list in visual design is a visual representation of text data. This is typically used to depict the keyword metadata (tags) on websites or to visualize the free form text. Tags are usually single words, and the importance of each tag is represented by font size or color.

2. Select **Brand** as **Word**, **Shipped Items** as **Word Color**, and **Revenue** as **Word Weight**.

3. Rename the visualization as **Unicorn Fashion Brands**.

    As a result, we will get this tag cloud:

The tag cloud visualization gives us a brief overview of the most popular brands based on the quantity of shipped items.

Creating a radar chart

Let's take a look at one more interesting chart, the radar chart:

A radar chart is a graphical method of displaying multivariate data in the form of a two-dimensional chart of three or more quantitative variables represented on axes starting from the same point. The relative position and angle of the axes is typically uninformative.

1. Select **Radar Chart** in visualization tools.
2. Then select **Revenue** as **Y Axis** and **Shipping City Name** as **Radar Branches**.

   As a result, we will get this chart:

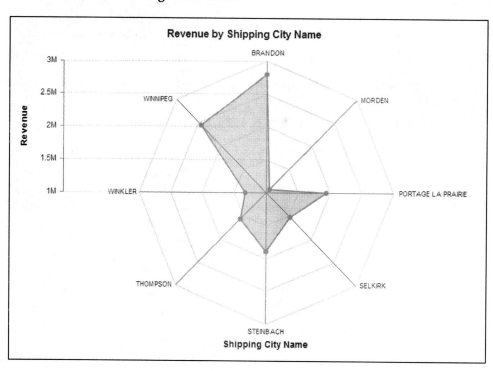

Now we can easily identify that **Winnipeg** and **Brandon** have the highest revenue. Moreover, we can compare revenue across cities.

At the end, it is a good idea to save our charts as Business Analytics.

Composing the data tab

SAP Lumira offers us several options to build valuable data stories or create data infographic, which describe our data using charts, texts, and images.

Let's go through the **Compose** tab and discover the possible options for creating stories in SAP Lumira. The **Compose** tab offers the following options:

- **Board**: This is organized into one or multiple sections. Each section can be used to add and format a chart, along with its own annotations, pictures, and active filters. Select a template that suits how you want to lay out your page.
- **Infographic**: This can be used to present an information flow or relationships between visualizations. You can combine various data visualizations with text information in order to provide the complete story.
- **Report**: This is a pixel-perfect rendering of the visualizations and other objects on the page. This is suitable for publishing and sharing. We can add any elements to the report.

Creating a Unicorn Fashion infographic

Once we have created visualizations, we can combine them into storyboards that group the information in a meaningful way.

Despite the fact that SAP Lumira offers us three different options to compose our data visualization, which are board, infographic, and report, we will take a look at only one because they are all based on the same idea.

Let's do it. Perform the following steps:

1. Click on **Compose** and the **Compose** tab will appear.

2. Select **Infographic** and enter the name as `Unicorn Fashion Overview`:

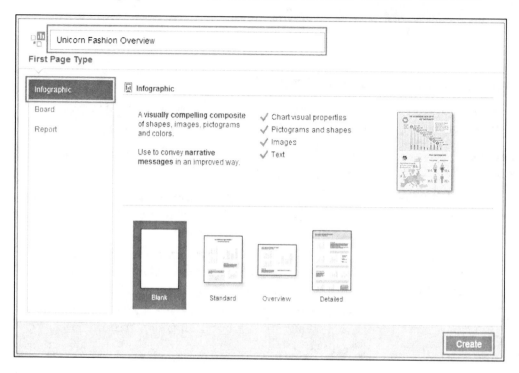

Based on the best practice, we should start any infographic, complex report, or dashboard from scratch, which we can draw by pencil.

3. Select **Standard Template** and enter the name as `Unicorn Fashion Overview`. Here, the smaller text is **Manitoba online fashion retailer**:

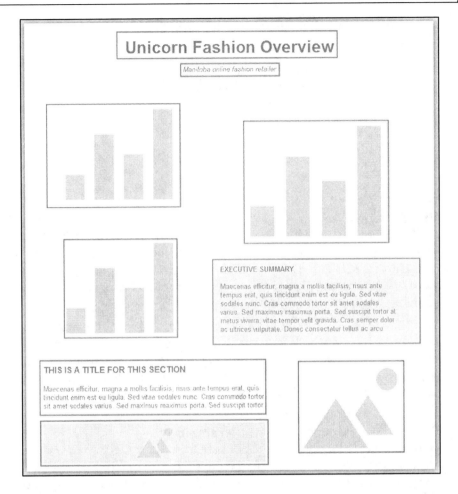

It consists of nine elements. We can easily replace or resize any of these elements. For example, we could select a blank list and add any objects to the sheet.

SAP Lumira give you the following options to work with your story. Let's take a look at them:

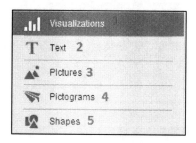

- **Visualizations (1):** This specifies all the available charts that are listed in the gallery before the tab. Drag a chart from the gallery to the board. A blue guide box shows the chart's placement on the board. After dropping a chart on the board, you can resize the chart. Charts added to a board are updated when the chart is modified in the visualize room. However, charts added to an infographic are not updated.

- **Text (2):** This allows you to drag the simple text, title, or the annotation text option from the gallery to the board. A blue guide box shows the box's placement on the board. After dropping a textbox on the board, you can enter text in the box. We can use chart customization to customize a bar, line, or column with pictogram and infochart customization for bar charts, column charts, line charts, and donut charts.

- **Pictures (3):** This denotes all the available images that are listed in the gallery before the tab. When you drag an image from the gallery to the board, a blue guide box shows the image's placement on the board. To add `.jpg`, `.jpeg`, `.png`, or `.gif` pictures to the gallery, click on the + icon at the top of the gallery. You can then search for images on your computer and add them to the gallery.

- **Pictograms (4):** This allows you to drag a plain `.svg` pictogram from the gallery to the board. A blue guide box shows the icon's placement on the board. Icons and symbols are listed in theme categories in the gallery before the tab.

- **Shapes (5):** This allows you to drag a plain `.svg` shape from the gallery to the board. A blue guide box shows the shape's placement on the board. Polygons and lines are listed in theme categories in the gallery before the tab.

Adding pictures

There is a logo of Unicorn Fashion in the attachment with this folder. Let's add it to our infographic using the following steps:

1. First, click on **Pictures**.

2. Then click on + and look for `Unicorn_logo.png` and `Manitoba_map.png`.

3. Next drag the logo to the bottom of the template.

4. Then drag the map to the template instead of one of the charts.

Adding visualizations

We can add any visualization which we have already done in this chapter, or we can go back to the visualize tab and create a new one. For example, the new tag cloud based on **Shipping City**.

Let's add our visualization to the template. Perform the following steps:

1. Click on **Visualizations**.

2. Drag and drop the tag cloud onto the template.

3. Navigate to the **Visualization Properties** section:

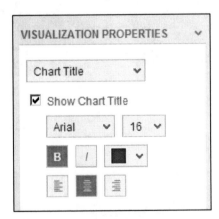

Visualization properties are available for all types of objects. It allows you to configure various parameters to make your infographic more interesting and beautiful. Perform the following steps:

1. First, uncheck **Chart Title** and **Legends**.

2. Then add **Top brands by Revenue**, but, before this, we have to go back to the visualize tab and change the rank filter from **10** to **3** because the top three brands will fit much better.

3. Uncheck **Chart Title** and **Legends**.

4. At the bottom of the template, add **Shipped Items by Order Date** and **Shipping City Name,** and configure the visualization option to fit this chart.

Adding text

There are two templates for text in our infographic; let's fill them with text. In addition, it is possible to change the font options in **Text Properties**.

As a result, we will get the following infographic:

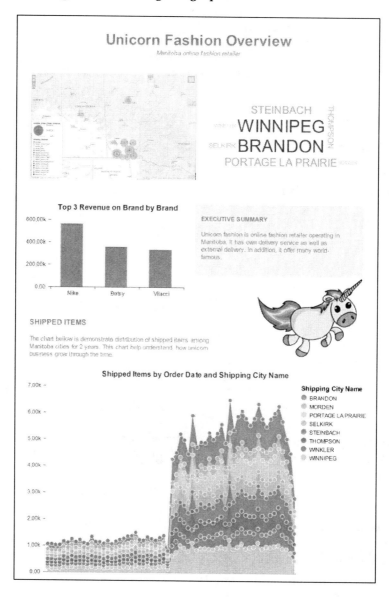

It is not that great, but it gives us an idea of how to create an infographic via SAP Lumira. Do not forget to save your work.

Summary

In this chapter, you have learned about the core functionality of SAP Lumira: visualizations. We have looked at various charts, such as column, radar, area, and so on. This gives us infinite capabilities to tell a story based on data. In addition, we have also looked at different types of charts, which give additional advantages for business analytics, such as sorting, ranking, and filtering. We have also looked at the external geo service. This allows you to work with geo data and create useful geo visualizations. Finally, we have tried to compose all our data visualizations via SAP Lumira, which allows us to create powerful infographic. In the next chapter, you will learn how to share your data visualization via various channels, such as e-mail or SAP applications.

5
Rocking Your Data in the Sky – SAP Lumira Cloud

The modern world requires very high standards for analytical software. It has to solve any big data analytics issue with the right tool. Most vendors shift their analytical solution to the cloud in order to add flexibility and power. This provides several advantages during the data discovery process and eliminates any struggle with software or hardware, which has very high standards in order to handle vast data. In addition, it reduces the expenditure on technology infrastructure and globalizes our workforce.

In this chapter, we will cover the following topics:

- Various data visualization techniques of SAP Lumira Cloud
- How to tell stories based on our data in the cloud
- How to create attractive infographics in the cloud

Getting started with SAP Lumira Cloud

SAP Lumira Cloud is a cloud application that provides us with capabilities to explore data, create dashboards, and tell stories. We can perform all this from web browsers or mobile devices and share it with others.

SAP Lumira Cloud allows you to perform the following actions:

- Create, explore, and share datasets and analytics via web browsers or mobile devices
- Share data visualization with teammates, colleagues, and publicity

- Import datasets from SAP Lumira
- Upload and share Crystal Reports documents, Design Studio files, Microsoft Excel spreadsheets, CSV files, ZIP files, or PowerPoint presentations

System requirements

Before we start to work with Lumira Cloud, we should check whether our browser or operation system is suitable for analysis. Let's view the system requirements in the following table:

Device	Operating System	Web Browser
Computer	Microsoft Windows	Internet Explorer, Safari, or Chrome
iPad	iOS7	Safari

If we are okay with the system requirements, we can start to register an account for Lumira Cloud.

Supported types of files

By default, in SAP Lumira Cloud, we can create new datasets based on flat files, such as CSV or Excel. Moreover, we can publish our visualizations and stories from SAP Lumira or just upload the Lumira documents. Lumira Cloud can work with the following file types:

- Design Studio files
- PowerPoint Presentations
- SAP Crystal Reports

Registering an account

From the SAP Lumira Cloud landing page, we can register for a free personal account, which provides 1 GB of free storage, in which we can upload and explore data. Let's register for a new SAP Lumira Cloud account. Perform the following steps:

1. Navigate to `https://cloud.saplumira.com/`.

2. Click on **Register New Account**. We need to enter the appropriate data in the required fields, which are flagged with an asterisk:

Before completing our registration, we need to review and accept the terms and conditions of using SAP Lumira Cloud. Fill the form and click on **Register**.

Now, we will get a message that our registration is now complete and an account has been created. Next, we will have to activate our account by clicking on the link that was sent to our e-mail account.

3. A confirmation e-mail will be sent to the e-mail address specified in the registration process. We should follow the instructions provided to activate the account.

4. Review the details for our account, set a password, and save the changes.

After the registration is successful, we can log in to SAP Lumira Cloud.

The SAP Lumira Cloud settings

On the **Account Info** tab, we can review the usage for our account. Information is also provided on how to upgrade to the SAP Lumira Cloud Enterprise edition, which enables us to share our content with colleagues. Let's take a look at the Lumira Cloud settings. Perform the following steps:

1. First, click on **Settings**. Then, on the **Profile** tab, we can update our account information with additional details:

2. Now, click on **Account Info**. On the **Account info** tab, we can review the usage for our account. Information is also provided on how to upgrade to the SAP Lumira Cloud Enterprise edition:

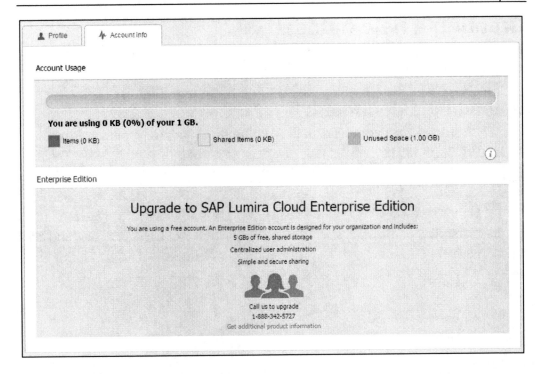

An Enterprise edition account has multiple GBs of shared storage. In addition, it is possible to manage the user security.

Introducing the SAP Lumira Cloud interface

When we log on to SAP Lumira Cloud, the following interface will appear:

There are two main components here:

- **My Items**: This specifies the tab that works with various data files. It has three columns: **Name, Owner,** and **Last Modified.** These provide information about the data file. Moreover, we can upload files to Lumira Cloud or create a new dataset based on CSV or Excel.

- **Settings**: This allows you to manage your profile and check the consumption of space for you or your team.

Creating a new dataset

We can continue to explore the interface and the capabilities of Lumira Cloud by creating a data visualization. Let's create one.

Uploading a document

In order to create a data visualization in SAP Lumira Cloud, we should upload a file with data. We can upload the data in the CSV or Excel file format. Let's start to create a small report based on extraction from the logistic module of the ERP system. Perform the following steps:

1. First, navigate to **My Items** and click on **Create Dataset**.
2. Then, click on **Browse**, select `Shipping Method Performance.csv`, and click on **Acquire**:

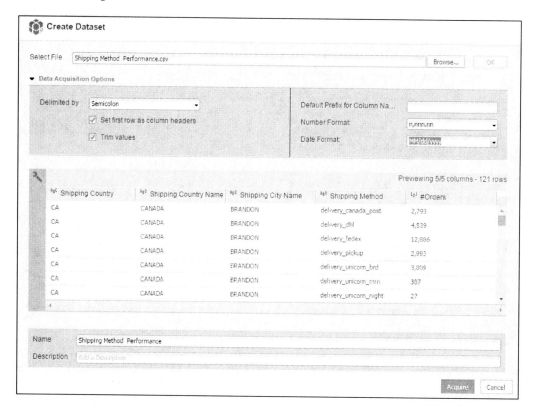

The **Visualize** window will appear.

Introducing the visualize tab

You learned a lot about the functionality of this tab in *Chapter 4, Visualizing Data and Telling Stories with It*. Therefore, we will just create a new visualization based on our data with the following steps:

1. First, select **Stacked Column Chart** in the chart builder.

2. Then, select **Orders** as **Y Axis**, **Shipping City Name** as **X Axis**, and **Shipping Method** as **Legend Color**.

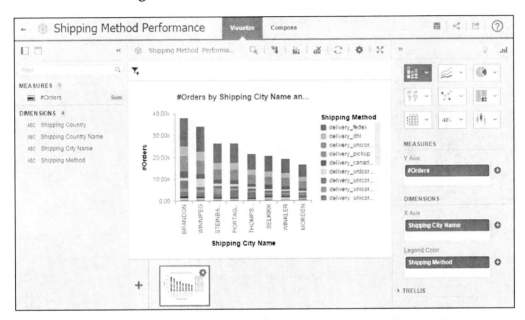

As a result, we can quickly analyze the performance of various shipping methods by cities. We figured out that for this particular period, **Brandon** has the most orders, and FedEx is a top shipping method for locations across Manitoba. The Unicorn Fashion COO has to improve the company's own delivery across Manitoba.

Composing the data visualization

Let's finish our report by clicking on **Compose**. We came across this tab in *Chapter 4, Visualizing Data and Telling Stories with It*. Create the report, as shown in the following screenshot:

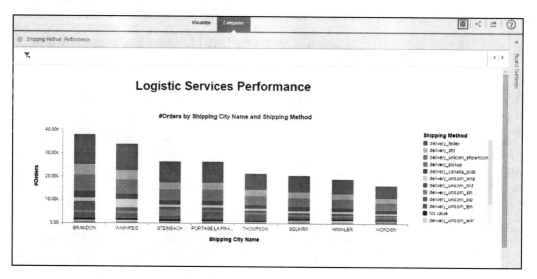

Now, save it as **Logistic Services Performance**.

As an analyst, we can easily build a business report by connecting to the Internet. In addition, we can share our visualization via the Web.

Creating a public report

SAP Lumira Cloud allows you to create a report, make a data story public, or just share it with your team if you have confidential data.

Let's try to make our **Logistic Services Performance** report public and embed it in a web page. Perform the following steps:

1. Navigate to **My Items** and click on the properties of our report, as shown in the following screenshot:

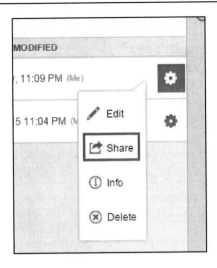

2. A new window will appear, where we can change the access rights.

3. Now, click on **Change Access**.

4. Then, select the **Public** option and click on **Save**.

5. Copy the URL for the report and paste it into the code for our web page:

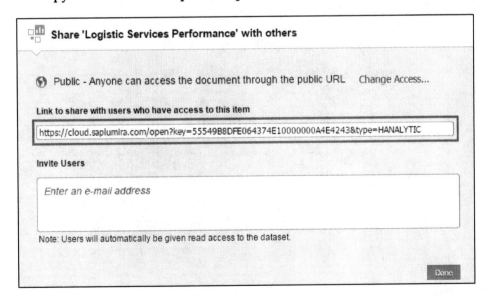

Then, click on **Done**. As a result, a global icon and the associated dataset will appear after the report to indicate that they are now public. Next, we will paste the link into the code for the web page.

6. Create a new text document as follows:

```
1   <!DOCTYPE HTML PUBLIC "-//W3C//DTD HTML 4.01//EN"
2        "http://www.w3.org/TR/html4/strict.dtd">
3   <html>
4       <head>
5       <title>Logistic Services Performance</title>
6       </head>
7   <body>
8   <iframe src="
    https://cloud.saplumira.com/open?key=55549B8DFE064374E10000000A4E4243&type=HANALYTIC"
    height="600" width="1250"></iframe>
9   </body>
10  </html>
```

Note that the tag for an IFrame is already defined, including the **height** and **width** for the frame. You can find more information about IFrame at http://www.w3schools.com/tags/tag_iframe.asp.

We should assign the URL of this report in the `src` parameter. Perform the following steps:

1. Save the document as `index.html`.

2. Open `index.html` to display the report in the IFrame for the test page, as shown in the following screenshot:

As a result, we can take a look at the core functionality of creating datasets and sharing it. Let's view the additional options. These can be useful for teamwork.

Teamwork in SAP Lumira Cloud

SAP Lumira Cloud is a powerful tool that can provide self-service BI for a small organization or any department in a large organization. In addition, it can complement traditional enterprise BI, especially SAP BusinessObjects.

When we have many users, the question of security and data access becomes urgent. That's why SAP Lumira Cloud offers extended security options for the Enterprise edition. For example, somebody in your organization can take the owner role and invite people to join the team. Ordinary members can work with data, create data visualizations, and share the result of analysis. Let's take a look at the various roles of Lumira Cloud.

The roles of a team

The free edition of SAP Lumira Cloud is restricted for security purposes. However, the Enterprise version allows you to create and assign various roles for Lumira users. The following table gives us a brief overview of all the possible roles:

Role	Actions
Member	This e-mails the team or individual members
Admin	This adds and removes members and e-mails the team or individual members
Owner	This adds and removes administrators and members and e-mails the team or individual members

Managing a team

In order to create a team or manage our existing team, we should navigate to the **Settings** tab. Here, we can perform all the actions related to security:

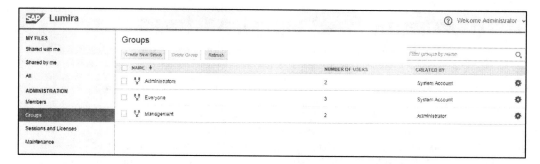

 This option will be available only for the Enterprise edition

The SAP Lumira Cloud mobile

Like any cloud application, SAP Lumira Cloud is available in the iPad. There are two possible options:

1. Download the SAP BusinessObjects mobile application from the App Store.

 You can find more information about this mobile application at `http://help.sap.com/bomobile`.

2. Download via the Safari browser: In this case, we also should visit `https://cloud.saplumira.com`. It has the same interface with one small difference, that is, the data panel is available in the list layout. Moreover, we will use our fingers instead of the mouse.

Summary

In this chapter, we looked at SAP Lumira Cloud. This is a cloud-based analytical solution that gives us flexibility. You learned about the system requirements and capabilities of Lumira Cloud. In addition, we created the data visualization and made it public with an embedded web page. We also discussed security options and roles. Finally, we looked at the Lumira solution for iPad.

In the next chapter, we will extend the capabilities of Lumira via customization, In addition, you will learn about the administration duties of SAP Lumira.

6
Administrating and Customizing SAP Lumira

The modern world is so complicated. Very often, there are not enough default options to analyze or visualize complex datasets and discover non-trivial patterns. You have learned a lot about SAP Lumira from the perspective of a user. For example, we have connected various data sources, prepared data, visualized data, and shared it. Moreover, we looked at cloud-based Lumira, which is very powerful and flexible. However, it is only a part of the whole picture. That's why in this chapter we will try to focus on more advance topics. This will help us to add more power to our data visualization by customizing charts and using various extensions. In addition, you will learn how to increase the computing capability of SAP Lumira by sizing the main parameters of Lumira.

Introducing the SAP Lumira administration

As with any analytical software, SAP Lumira will require administration attention. Despite the fact that Lumira is an end user application and designed to be user friendly, you should learn a little bit about useful capabilities that can help us on our way to become a data geek.

Updating SAP Lumira

SAP is a modern company. It tries to improve and develop its products. We can choose the updating method, such as manual or automatic.

We can check for an update in order to get the last version. We should click on **Help | Check for updates**, as shown in the following screenshot:

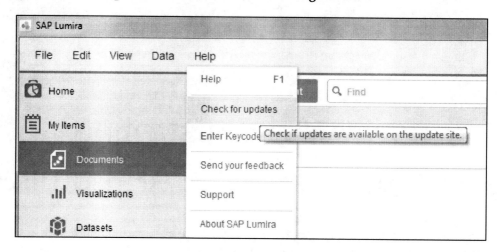

As a result, SAP Lumira will check for updates and offer it if available.

 You can learn more about the latest version of SAP Lumira at http://scn.sap.com/community/lumira.

Moreover, we can also set up the frequency of updates. Navigate to **File> Preference > Software Updates**:

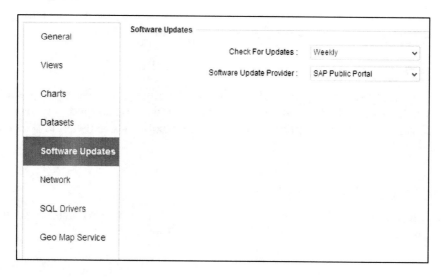

There are two software update providers:

- SAP Support Portal
- SAP Public Portal

You can find a lot of addition information in the installation manual at http://help. sap.com/businessobject/product_guides/vi01/en/lum_125_install_en.pdf.

Uninstalling SAP Lumira

We can easily delete SAP Lumira as any other software but only if we have admin rights for the computer. Otherwise, we should ask our system administrator to update or delete SAP Lumira. As any other Windows-based applications, we can delete it from **Control Panel**.

Sizing SAP Lumira

Usually, when we install analytical software, it has settings by default and in most cases these default settings are not appropriate, especially for data analytics. As a result, you should learn how to install SAP Lumira in order to analyse massive data.

There are several useful options, such as memory settings, multiuser sizing, RAM sizing, and disk sizing. Let's take a look at all of them.

Adjusting memory settings

Sometimes, users have to process a large data file. As a result, they can get errors related to limited RAM resources. If we get an issue with RAM, we can fix it by navigating to `<SAP Lumira Folder>\SAP Lumira\Desktop\SAPLumira.ini`. We should open this file with a text editor, as shown in the following screenshot:

```
SAPLumira.ini
 1    -startup
 2    plugins/org.eclipse.equinox.launcher_1.3.0.v20120522-1813.jar
 3    --launcher.library
 4    plugins/org.eclipse.equinox.launcher.win32.win32.x86_64_1.1.200.v20120913-144807
 5    --launcher.appendVmargs
 6    -vmargs
 7    -Xmx1024m
 8    -XX:MaxPermSize=128M
 9    -XX:+CMSClassUnloadingEnabled
10    -XX:+UseConcMarkSweepGC
11    -Dhilo.shared.dir.name=sapvi
12    -Dhilo.maxvizdatasetsize=10000
13    -Dhilo.cef.cache.enabled=true
14    -Dosgi.instance.area=@user.home/.sapvi/workspace
15    -Dosgi.configuration.area=@user.home/.sapvi/configuration
16    -Dosgi.checkConfiguration=true
17    -Dhilo.auto.recovery.enabled=true
18    -Dhilo.user.dir=@user.home/.sapvi
19    -Dorg.osgi.framework.os.name=win32
```

By default, SAP Lumira has `-Xmx1024 m` and `-Dhilo.maxvizdatasetsize= 10000` rows.

- `-Dhilo.maxvizdatasetsize`: This specifies the maximum number of data points permitted in a chart before a message appears, advising you to filter or rank the values to reduce the data points. You can increase this value to increase the threshold.

- `-Xmx`: This denotes the virtual memory allocated to the application.

 The parameter name was called *hilo* because the project name of Lumira was called Hilo, a city of Hawaii.

However, we can increase it. For example, it is possible to increase the `-xmx` parameter until 25-50 percent of our RAM. Moreover, the best way is to start from the default size and in case of any problem increase both the parameters.

Multiuser sizing of SAP Lumira

Often organizations prefer to use one power computer and organize remote access via Citrix or Windows services. This approach can save money because a company can reduce the usage of license per machine and the number of expensive machines as well. In addition, it is possible to hold Lumira in the same data center as the data stored. It gives additional advantages due to better latency and quicker response. There are two methods for multiuser access:

- Create virtual machines for every user with separate SAP Lumira
- Support many parallel sessions for SAP Lumira

Both these methods can be sized. For example, when we have many sessions on one machine, we should adjust the memory in such a way that every user has enough resources for his/her tasks. In other words, we should multiply the number of potential users on RAM. Another important topic is the size of disk; we should calculate the size as well.

There are some best practices of multiuser sizing:

- 4 GB RAM per user
- 150 MB of free space per user

Getting started with the SAP Lumira SDK

SAP Lumira can become a very powerful tool with custom visualizations or custom data sources. It allows you to develop custom visualizations with the SAP VizPacker visualization utility as well as create data access extension to access out-of-the box data sources. The development of this new extension is not so easy and requires knowledge of some of the following technologies:

- JavaScript

 A good tutorial on JavaScript is available at: `http://www.w3schools.com/js/default.asp`.

- HTML5

 A good tutorial on HTML5 is available at `http://www.w3schools.com/html/default.asp`.

- jQuery
- CSS

 A good tutorial on CSS is available at `http://www.w3schools.com/css/default.asp`.

- D3 (Data-Driven Documents)

 Lots of custom visualization is based on the open source data visualization library. There are some useful books on `D3.js` at `https://www.packtpub.com/web-development/data-visualization-d3js-cookbook` and `https://www.packtpub.com/web-development/data-visualization-d3js`.

- The SAP web IDE

For example, I am not a software engineer. That's why I want to show you how to use a Lumira extension that is based on VizPacker without any programming. In this case, we should start from the SAP Lumira visualization library.

Meeting SAP Lumira's data visualization library

We can find the predefined custom data visualization in GitHub at `https://github.com/SAP/lumira-extension-viz`.

There are several data visualizations you can use for your data:

- **Hello World**: This is the extension from which you can learn how VizPacker works:

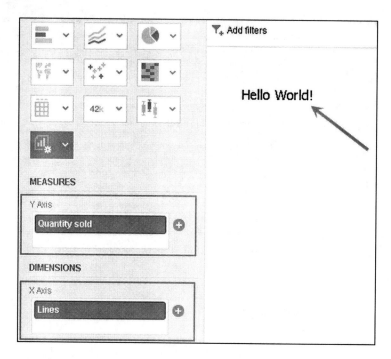

> You can find more information on how to create **Hello World** at `http://scn.sap.com/community/lumira/blog/2013/12/19/hello-world-extension-for-sap-lumira`.

- **The Bullet chart**: This is useful when we want to represent a lot of measures on one bar chart. We can use it when want to represent **Revenue** versus the plan revenue with additional parameters.

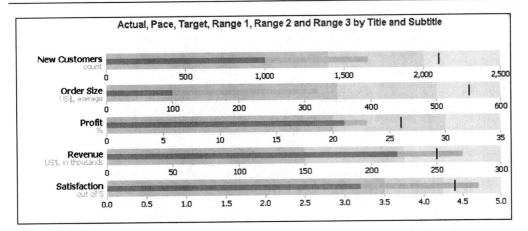

 You can find more information at `http://bl.ocks.org/mbostock/4061961`.

- **Exoplanets**: This chart allows you to represent data in bubbles based on radius, distance, and name:

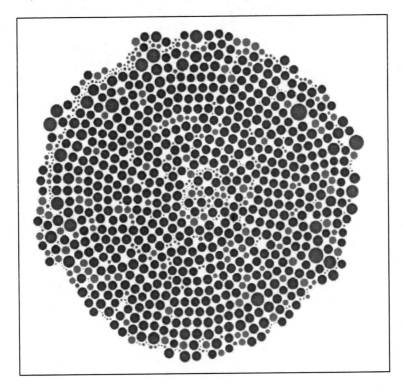

You can find more information at `http://bl.ocks.org/ mbostock/3007180`.

- **The Population Pyramid chart**: The name of this chart tells us when this chart can be useful. This particular chart represents the distribution of population by year, age, gender:

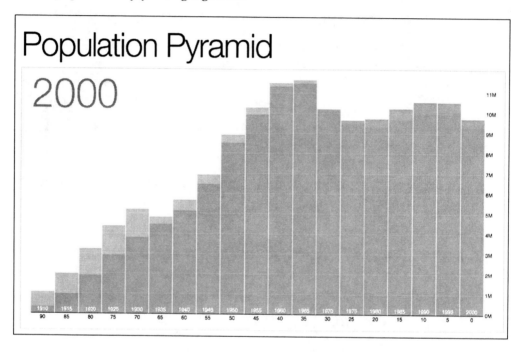

 You can find more information at `http://bl.ocks.org/ mbostock/4062085`.

- **The Force diagram**: This represents the connections between networked entities. This diagram is useful when we want to show relations among people in social networks:

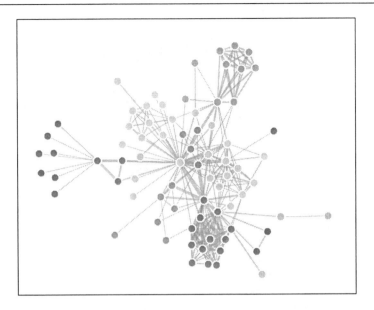

[💡 You can find more information at `http://bl.ocks.org/`
`mbostock/4062045`.]

- **The Stacked Column with Line chart**: This chart overlays a line on top of the stacked bar chart and is based on the `D3.js` visualization:

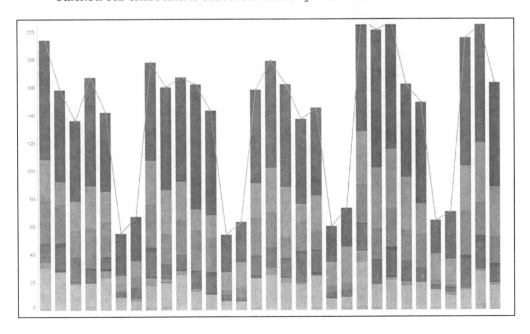

You can find this chart at `http://bl.ocks.org/otfrom/4754261`.

- **Google Maps Heat map**: This allows you to use geo data in order to draw the heat map based on our data:

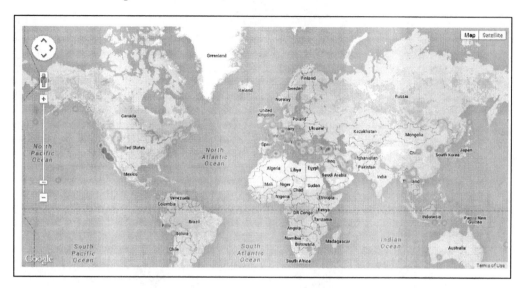

 You can find more information on how to create a heat map via Google Maps at `http://scn.sap.com/community/lumira/blog/2014/12/04/analyzin-world-earthquakes-on-google-heatmap-extension-for-lumira`.

- **Mini charts**: This can be used to create information panels for the management team because it allows you to represent many charts in one screen and gives you more power in the decision-making process, as shown in the following image:

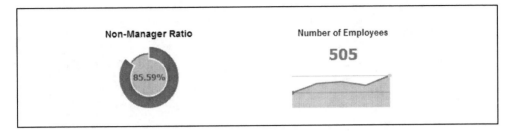

 You can find more information on how to create mini charts at `http://scn.sap.com/community/lumira/blog/2015/01/27/fiori-like-lumira-extensions-mini-charts`.

- **Custom Predictive charts**: SAP Lumira allows you to use statistics and machine learning in order to build forecasting models. Let's take a look at some popular examples:
  - The forecast chart with single confidence interval:

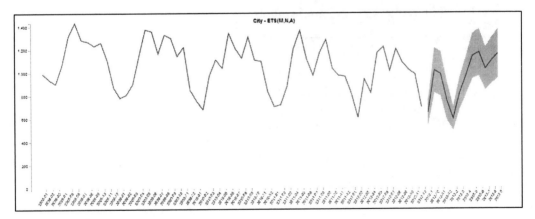

○ The forecast chart with 80 percent and 95 percent confidence intervals:

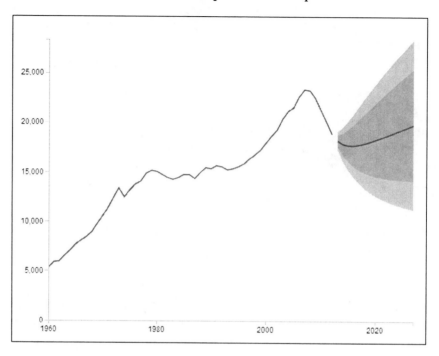

• The Holt-Winters exponential smoothing chart:

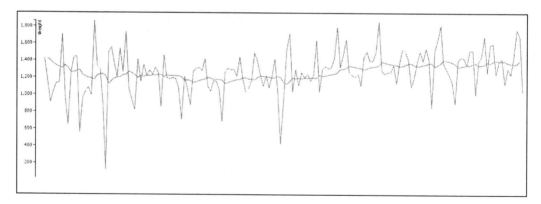

 You can find more details about these charts with predictive flavour at
http://scn.sap.com/community/lumira/blog/2015/01/27/
sap-lumira-chart-extensions-with-a-predictive-flavor.

Deploying a custom extension

Let's try to use one of the custom charts from the GitHub library to visualize the shipping data. Perform the following steps:

1. Check whether you have SAP Lumira version 1.25 or higher. If not, then you should update it.

2. Go to `https://github.com/SAP/lumira-extension-viz` and click on **Download Zip**. The library will be downloaded.

3. Then, extract the library from the archive.

4. Now run SAP Lumira.

5. Then click on **File> Extensions** and then **Manual Installation**.

6. Find the extracted folder and select **Chord Chart** or any other chart.

7. Now restart SAP Lumira.

8. Click on **File> New**, select flat files, navigate to the Chord data viz folder, and select `hair.csv`:

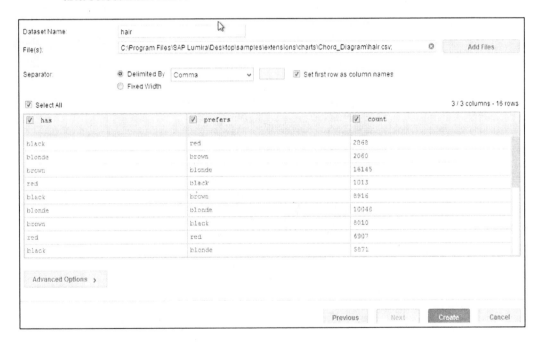

9. Click on **Create** and the Lumira **Visualize** tab will appear.

10. There is a new chart option with custom extensions available in the charts toolbar. Select **Chord Chart**:

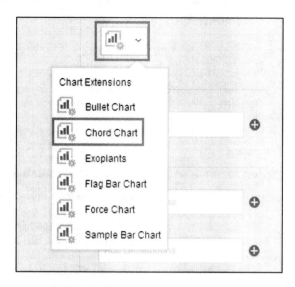

11. Drag and drop **count** to **Measures** and **has** along with **prefers** to **Dimensions**:

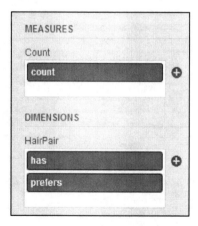

12. As a result, the chord chart will be drawn as follows:

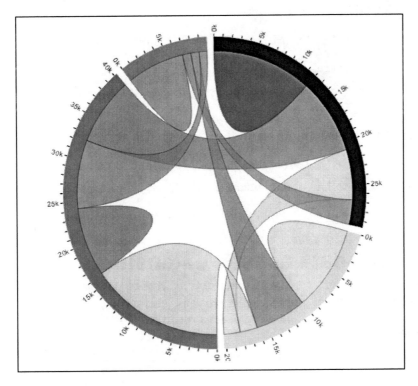

 The chord chart is a very popular chart. It represents directed relationships among various entities. You can find more information at http://bl.ocks.org/mbostock/4062006.

Creating a new extension

You have already learned how to use Lumira extensions. However, you can also create your own extension based on D3.js or any other visualization.

The best way is to start with Lumira. You can learn how to develop an extension at http://scn.sap.com/docs/DOC-61422v.

Moreover, you can start to develop your extension based on a step-by-step guide available at the following links:

- *How to add a D3.js extension for SAP Lumira by Matt Lloyd* (http://scn.sap.com/community/lumira/blog/2014/02/19/how-to-add-a-d3-extension-for-sap-lumira)

- *Create cool SAP Lumira visualization extensions with the SAP web IDE* by Dong Pan (https://www.youtube.com/watch?v=ZbWUVhoCLto)

In addition, you can learn more about the SAP web IDE at:

- The SAP web IDE – Analytics (http://scn.sap.com/docs/DOC-63081)
- The SAP web IDE – Enablement (http://scn.sap.com/docs/DOC-55465)

These resources give us a detailed overview of the Lumira customization.

Creating a data access extension

SAP Lumira allows you to create an extension to access a new source of data, which is not available by default. For example, we can create a connector to XML, Google Spreadsheet, Twitter, or any other data. As a result, we got a new source: the **External Datasource**:

Let's learn how Lumira can create a new data visualization based on the data access extension. Perform the following steps:

1. First, click on **File> New** and select **External Datasource**.
2. Then, click on **Next**; we will get all the available extensions. Select one.
3. We should choose a file through the user interface.
4. We can preview the data by clicking on the **Preview** button.
5. Now, click on **Create** and the data will be imported.

As a result, the data access extension will work in a similar way to the original data source.

You can learn how to develop your own data access extension by referring to the following resources:

*   Guide to SAP Lumira data access extensions (`http://scn.sap.com/community/lumira/blog/2014/09/24/my-personal-guide-to-sap-lumira-data-access-extensions`)
*   Data access extension for Twitter data (`http://scn.sap.com/community/lumira/blog/2014/09/12/a-lumira-extension-to-acquire-twitter-data`)
*   Data access extension for MS Access (`http://scn.sap.com/community/lumira/blog/2014/09/26/a-better-aproach-to-ms-access-lumira-msaccess-extension-dae`)

Summary

In this chapter, we looked at various SAP Lumira parameters, which are important when we are working with big data. In other words, you learned about Lumira from the administrator perspective. In addition, you learned about the capabilities of the SAP Lumira customization, such as how to create new visualization or data access extensions. We also looked at the SAP Lumira visualization library. It provides us with ready-to-use custom visualizations. In the next chapter, we will take a look at the connection between SAP Lumira, SAP HANA, and SAP BusinessObjects.

7
Connecting to SAP BusinessObjects BI Platform and SAP HANA

SAP solutions are very popular among international companies. Most of them have various SAP products, which include business solutions, customer relationship management systems, enterprise resource planning systems, and business analytics systems, such as SAP BusinessObjects and SAP HANA.

SAP Lumira complements both systems and provides powerful analytics functions and extended data visualizations.

In this chapter, you will learn the following:

- How to connect to SAP BusinessObjects universe
- How to publish in SAP BusinessObjects Explorer and the SAP BI platform
- How to connect to SAP BusinessObjects HANA
- Restrictions of SAP connections

Introducing the SAP BusinessObjects BI platform

The SAP BusinessObjects BI platform (also known as BO or BOBI) is a part of the SAP Business Intelligence portfolio that allows business users to view, sort, and analyze business intelligence data. It is specially designed for enterprise reporting and has various modules, which cover the requirements of any organization.

SAP BusinessObjects consists of various modules designed for special purposes. The following image shows the SAP BusinessObjects BI platform:

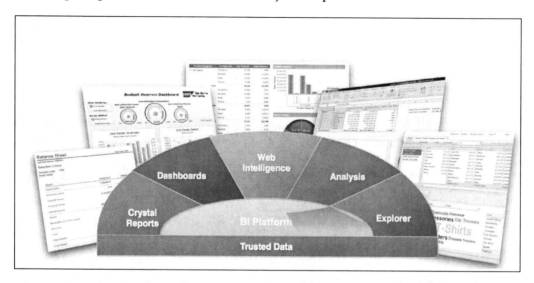

Let's take a look at the main products of the SAP BusinessObjects BI platform:

- **Crystal Reports**: This allows you to create pixel-perfect reports. For example, we can create tax reports.

- **Dashboards**: This allows you to create interactive dashboards with Flash and HTML5.

- **Web Intelligence**: This is the most popular tool. It allows you to create ad hoc reports.

- **Analysis**: This allows you to work with MOLAP cubes.

- **Explorer**: This allows you to create in-memory datasets for the purpose of data discovery.

You can find more information about the SAP BusinessObjects BI product portfolio at `http://blogs.sap.com/analytics/2014/06/25/` `run-simple-convergence-of-the-sap-businessobjects-bi-` `product-portfolio/`.

Many organizations prefer SAP BI platform as the primary BI tool for their needs. However, it lacks the visualization functionality. In addition, it is not suitable for data discovery, where we need to work with vast amounts of data by slicing and dicing it. Moreover, SAP BI clients are not designed for big data analytics and lack a self-service nature in data discovery. Fortunately, we have SAP Lumira which can complement the traditional BI tool (such as SAP BO). It offers rich functionalities and big data analytics.

There are two useful books on SAP BusinessObjects ready for us:

- Creating Universe with SAP BusinessObjects (`https://www.` `packtpub.com/big-data-and-business-intelligence/` `creating-universes-sap-businessobjects`)
- SAP BusinessObjects Reporting Cookbook (`https://www.` `packtpub.com/big-data-and-business-intelligence/` `sap-businessobjects-reporting-cookbook`)

Connecting to the SAP BO universe

Universe is a core thing in the SAP BusinessObjects BI platform. It is the semantic layer that isolates business users from the technical complexities of the databases where their corporate information is stored. For the ease of the end user, universes are made up of objects and classes that map to data in the database, using everyday terms that describe their business environment.

Introducing the Unicorn Fashion universe

The Unicorn Fashion company uses the SAP BusinessObjects BI platform (BIP) as its primary BI tool. We already looked at its datamart in *Chapter 2, Connecting to Data Sources*. There is another Unicorn Fashion universe, which was built based on the unicorn datamart. It has a similar structure and joins as datamart. The following image shows the Unicorn Fashion universe:

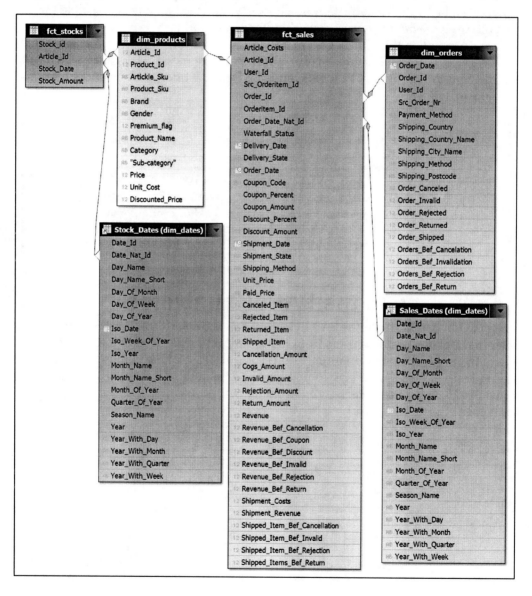

It unites two business processes: **Sales** (orange) and **Stock** (green) and has the following structure in business layer:

- **Product**: This specifies the attributes of an SKU, such as brand, category, ant, and so on
  - ° **Price**: This denotes the different pricing of the SKU

- **Sales**: This specifies the sales business process
  - ° **Order**: This denotes the order number, the shipping information, and orders measures
  - ° **Sales Date**: This specifies the attributes of order date, such as month, year, and so on
  - ° **Sales Measures**: This denotes various aggregated measures, such as shipped items, revenue waterfall, and so on

- **Stock**: This specifies the information about the quantity on stock
  - ° **Stock Date**: This denotes the attributes of stock date, such as month, year, and so on

Import the universe to SAP BO

There is an archive lcmbiar (Unicorn Fashion Universe.lcmbiar) provided with the code bundle of this chapter. Let's import universe in the existing SAP BIP server using the following steps:

1. Navigate to **Central Management Console** of SAP BO.

2. Then, go to **Promotion Management**, click on **Import**, and select Unicorn Fashion Universe.lcmbiar:

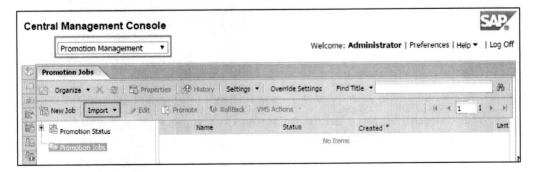

3. Log in to **SAP BO Server** and promote job.

As a result, we will import universe in the SAP BIP repository.

Supporting universes

SAP Lumira supported universes of SAP BusinessObjects 3.X and 4.X. It supported both types of universes: .unv and .unx.

Connecting to the Unicorn Fashion universe

We have successfully imported Unicorn Fashion universe in the SAP BO repository. As a result, we can connect it via SAP Lumira in order to create data visualization or report.

Let's try it. Perform the following steps:

1. Open SAP Lumira.

2. Click on **File>New**.

3. Select **Universe** as a source.

4. Enter the **Universe credentials** and click on **Connect**. In the following example, **System** is an example, and you should use your own system:

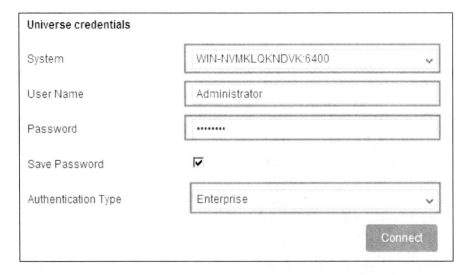

5. Find your universe in the Unicorn Fashion folder and click on **Next**.

6. Select **Result Objects: Brand, Shipping City Name, Revenue**, and **Shipped Item** and click on **Next**:

7. Our universe has many predefined filters. Navigate to **Filters**, select **Gender**,and click on **Next**.

8. In the previous step, we chose **Filters**. As a result, Lumira tells you to choose the gender for your answer set. Let's select **Female**, **Male**, and click on **Next**:

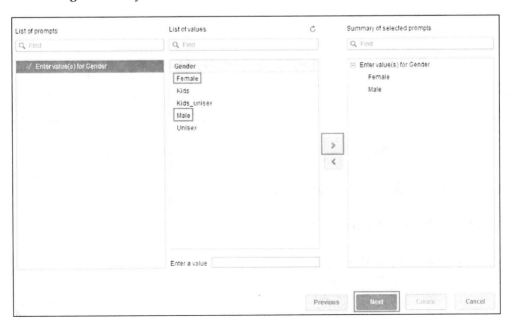

As a result, SAP Lumira created a SQL via universe and the universe sent it to the database, which then came back with the answer set. Let's create one more visualization based on our dataset.

Creating the bubble chart

Perform the following steps:

1. Select **Scatter Plot** in visualization tools.

2. Drag and drop the **Shipped Item** measure as **X Axis**, the **Revenue** measure as **Y Axis**, the **Brand** dimension as **Legend Color**, and the **Shipping City Name** dimension as **Legend Shape**:

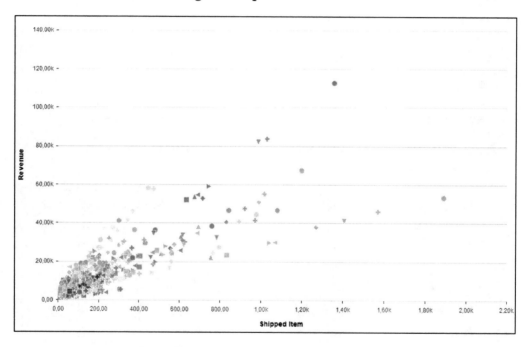

3. Then, save it as **Shipped Item** and **Revenue** by **City** and **Brand**.

4. As a result, we can see that most brands are grouped together. We can start slice and dice data in order to find new patterns and outliers.

Editing the data source

We can easily add dimensions or measures and change the values of filters by clicking on the **Data >Edit Data Source** or by pressing *Ctrl+Shift+E.*

Publishing the dataset or story to SAP BI

SAP Lumira allows you to publish the dataset or story to the SAP BI platform, where it will be visible in the BI launchpad. In order to perform this, we should add the setting to SAP Lumira **Preferences**. Let's try to publish our story to the SAP BI platform. Perform the following steps:

1. Navigate to **File>Preferences>Network** and type your server:

 The default port number for the RESTful web services is 6405.

2. Then, we should go to the **Share** tab, select the dataset or story, and click on **Publish to SAP BI**:

3. Enter the SAP BI credentials and click on **Publish**.

Troubleshooting tips for a universe

When we connect to a universe, we may encounter errors. There is a table with all the possible errors and causes:

Error message	Causes
Could not connect to Central Management Server (CMS)	This error might occur in the following scenarios: <ul><li>The CMS is down</li><li>The username or password is incorrect</li><li>The authentication type is incorrect</li><li>A network issue</li></ul>

Error message	Causes
Could not load the selected universe	This error might occur in the following scenarios: • An issue with the database connection • Mismatch of data types for the selected object • The result returned from the server reached the limit set for the configuration parameter — *Maximum Character Stream Size (MB) of Web Intelligence Report Server* • The universe object(s) is not configured properly
Could not validate the query	This error might occur in the following scenarios: • The universe is corrupted • The CMS is down • The universe connection is not configured properly
Query returns no row sets	The selected object(s) results in a query that returns empty data

Introducing SAP Explorer

The SAP BusinessObjects Explorer tool is designed to search data. This allows you to quickly and accurately obtain the answers to business questions on the basis of corporate data. With the help of search, you can find the necessary data in a coherent and meaningful dataset. This is known as the information space which allow us to discover our data set, use filters and create visualizations. When you work in the application, the user can perform visual analysis, which allows quick access to the necessary information in the most appropriate format.

SAP BusinessObjects Explorer provides an intuitive way to quickly find and analyze data to instantly get an idea of the state of affairs in the company. Any user BI solutions can easily find answers to pressing questions without training and the IT support staff—just enter a few keywords to search for the right information— intuitive analysis of large amounts of data, prior knowledge of the location of data, and their composition is not required.

Publishing the dataset in SAP Explorer

Unicorn Fashion has SAP BO as the enterprise BI and Explorer is a part of this BI. Some advance analytics play with datasets in SAP Lumira. In order to demonstrate the result to other BI users, they publish visualization in SAP Explorer. Let's try to perform it with the following steps:

1. Open our **Shipped Item** and **Revenue by City** and **Brand visualization**.

2. Click on the **Shipped Item** and **Revenue by City** and **Brand dataset**.

3. Then, click on **Publish to Explorer**:

4. Enter the CMS credentials.

5. Select the destination folder where the new information space will be created.

6. Then, click on **Publish**.

We have just created the new information space in SAP BO.

> Information space is a collection of objects mapped to data for a specific business operation or activity. The users of SAP BusinessObjects Explorer enter the keywords related to the business question they wish to analyze in order to retrieve the information space(s) that contain the relevant data. Power users along with the space creator user profile create the information space(s) on top of corporate data providers.

Let's check it:

1. Navigate to the BI launchpad and find the destination folder.
2. Open the Unicorn Fashion information space:

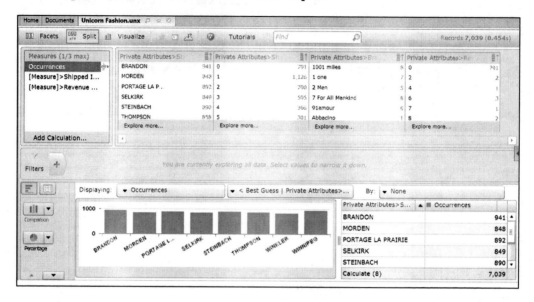

SAP Explorer has the visual data representation aimed to support data exploration. However, we can distribute our dataset and business insights across the organization.

Restriction to publishing in SAP Explorer

We should keep in mind some restrictions when you export a dataset to SAP Explorer:

Restriction	Description
Multiple members with identical captions	Distinct dimension members with the same caption in a dataset are merged into a single member at the SAP Explorer level when published. The following consequences are possible:
	Inconsistent location of data in a geographical dataset. For example, Russia (RU) and Moscow (MO) would be merged together.
	Inconsistent values in aggregated data. For example, Russia (RU) and Moscow (MO) would be merged into a single SAP Explorer member.
Unsupported measures	Measures that use aggregation functions that are not supported in SAP Explorer are not exported. SAP Explorer supports the none, sum, min, max, and count aggregation functions.

Restriction	Description
SAP HANA online datasets	It is not possible to export online datasets based on the SAP HANA views.
Date and number formats	The formats of date and number are not preserved during the export process. SAP Explorer applies its own formatting, irrespective of the original formatting options.
Geographical data	Dimension members that are flagged as unresolved during the reconciliation step are displayed as `<unresolved>` in SAP Explorer.
The size of exported dataset	A dataset with more than ten million cells cannot be published to SAP Explorer. If you have trouble publishing a large dataset (less than 10 million cells), there may be a memory limit set on the SAP Explorer indexing server.
Required SAP Explorer rights	Exporting a dataset to SAP Explorer requires the following special rights: • Permission to create an information space • Permission to index an information space • Permission to write to the selected folder

Introducing SAP HANA

SAP HANA is a high-performance platform for NewSQL data storage and processing. It is based on the computing technology in-memory and uses the principle of the columnar storage platform. This platform has been developed and brought to the market by SAP SE. The SAP HANA architecture provides high-speed transaction processing and works with complex analytic queries, combining these tasks on a single platform.

Except for the RDBMS, SAP HANA provides application services and integration services as well. SAP HANA applications can be created using the JavaScript code on the server side and the HTML code.

For more details, refer to `https://blogs.saphana.com/2015/04/28/sap-hana-platform-today/`.

There are two useful books on SAP HANA ready for us:

• SAP HANA Cookbook (`https://www.packtpub.com/big-data-and-business-intelligence/sap-hana-cookbook`)

• SAP HANA Starter (`https://www.packtpub.com/big-data-and-business-intelligence/sap-hana-starter-instant`)

Connecting to SAP HANA

There are two options to connect SAP Lumira to SAP HANA:

- **Connecting to SAP HANA**: This method allows you to connect data to the SAP HANA view

- **Downloading from SAP HANA**: This method allows you to download data from the SAP HANA view as a dataset

There are two options to learn and practice how to connect SAP Lumira via SAP HANA:

- Using the deployment of SAP HANA

- Using Cloud SAP HANA. In this case, we should refer to `https://aws.amazon.com/sap/solutions/saphana/`

   Cloud Appliance Library from SAP (`http://cal.sap.com`): This is considered to be the better starting point as it includes multiple HANA licensing options (including the free developer's edition) hosted by multiple cloud vendors, thereby giving a choice of subscription costs.

We will choose the deployment of SAP HANA in order to demonstrate how to connect to the SAP HANA view.

For example, we have two analytic views in SAP HANA:

- **STS_VIEW_OFFLINE**
- **STS_VIEW_ONLINE**

We can create a preview of the **STS_VIEW_ONLINE** data in SAP HANA as follows:

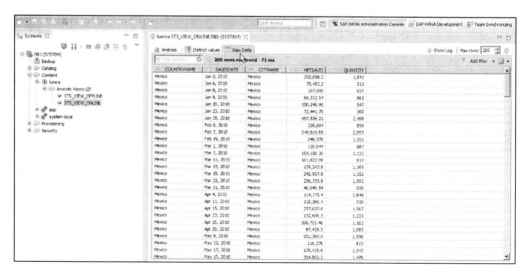

Let's try to connect the SAP HANA view via SAP Lumira with the following steps:

1. Open SAP Lumira.
2. Navigate to **File> New**.
3. Select **Connect** to SAP HANA as a datasource and click on **Next**:

4. Enter the credentials of SAP HANA and click on **Next**.
5. Select **STS_VIEW_ONLINE**, enter STS Online HANA View as **Dataset Name**, and click on **Next**:

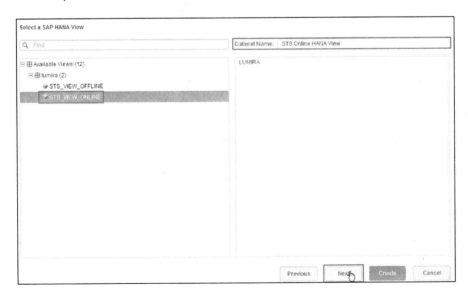

6. Use **Select Measures and Attributes** and click on **Create**:

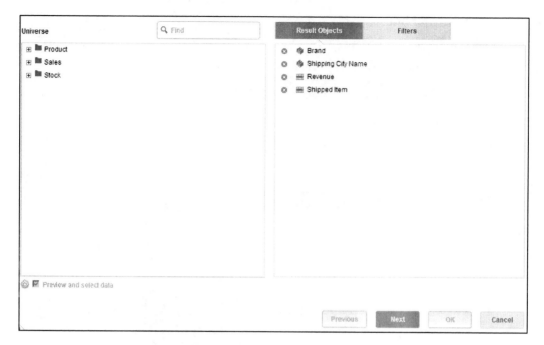

As a result, we can create a new dataset with data from SAP HANA, and we can create the new data visualization based on the SAP HANA data.

Restrictions for SAP HANA connections

There are some restrictions of the SAP HANA connection mentioned in the following table:

Restrictions	Descriptions
Only one level is available for geographical hierarchies	Only one attribute at a time can be used when you create a geographical hierarchy.
Measures with numeric or string dimensions cannot be created	Measures are detected from the SAP HANA analytic view. These must be created in the SAP HANA view before the application can automatically acquire them.
Datasets cannot be published to SAP HANA	It it impossible to publish dataset from SAP Lumira to SAP HANA

Restrictions	Descriptions
Some functions are not supported	The following SAP HANA functions are not supported: • AddMonthToDate • AddYearToDate • LastDayOfMonth • DayOfYear • Week • LastWord • Except LastWord
Some features are not available for analytic views that use a calculation view	When an analytic view uses a calculation view, for example, when an attribute view in the analytic view has a calculated measure or one or more calculated columns, the grid view is not available in the prepare room. When a measure is selected in the prepare room, facets do not show any values. Sorting on a measure is not possible in the visualize room.

Summary

In this chapter, we looked at the SAP Business Objects BI platform, SAP HANA, and discussed the role of SAP Lumira in the ecosystem of SAP analytical applications. We also created a visualization based on the Unicorn Fashion universe and published it to the SAP BI platform for our visualization. In addition, you learned SAP Explorer and created a new information space via SAP Lumira. Finally, we looked at how to connect SAP HANA online and acquire data from it.

Index

SDK, SAP Lumira
  about 109
  custom extension, deploying 117
  data access extension, creating 120, 121
  data visualization library 110-115
  new extension, creating 119, 120
Software as a Service (SaaS) 8
Stacked Column with Line Chart 113

T

tag cloud
  creating 81, 82
text files 28-30
time hierarchy 56

U

Unicorn Fashion infographic
  creating 83-86
  pictures, adding 86
  text, adding 88
  visualizations, adding 87
Unicorn Fashion universe
  about 17, 18, 126, 127
  importing, to SAP BO 127
Unicorn Fashion universe
  bubble chart, creating 130
  connecting 128-130
  data source, editing 130

V

visualization, building
  about 69
  area chart, creating 77
  column chart, creating 70
  fields, renaming 69, 70
  filter dimensions 75, 76
  geographic chart, creating 73, 74
  multiple charts, creating 78
  out-of-the-box chart, creating 81
  rank dimensions 71, 72
  sort order 71
visualization data tab
  about 66-68
  out-of-the-box charts, creating 81
  visualization, building 69

Thank you for buying
SAP Lumira Essentials

About Packt Publishing

Packt, pronounced 'packed', published its first book, *Mastering phpMyAdmin for Effective MySQL Management*, in April 2004, and subsequently continued to specialize in publishing highly focused books on specific technologies and solutions.

Our books and publications share the experiences of your fellow IT professionals in adapting and customizing today's systems, applications, and frameworks. Our solution-based books give you the knowledge and power to customize the software and technologies you're using to get the job done. Packt books are more specific and less general than the IT books you have seen in the past. Our unique business model allows us to bring you more focused information, giving you more of what you need to know, and less of what you don't.

Packt is a modern yet unique publishing company that focuses on producing quality, cutting-edge books for communities of developers, administrators, and newbies alike. For more information, please visit our website at www.packtpub.com.

About Packt Open Source

In 2010, Packt launched two new brands, Packt Open Source and Packt Enterprise, in order to continue its focus on specialization. This book is part of the Packt Open Source brand, home to books published on software built around open source licenses, and offering information to anybody from advanced developers to budding web designers. The Open Source brand also runs Packt's Open Source Royalty Scheme, by which Packt gives a royalty to each open source project about whose software a book is sold.

Writing for Packt

We welcome all inquiries from people who are interested in authoring. Book proposals should be sent to author@packtpub.com. If your book idea is still at an early stage and you would like to discuss it first before writing a formal book proposal, then please contact us; one of our commissioning editors will get in touch with you.

We're not just looking for published authors; if you have strong technical skills but no writing experience, our experienced editors can help you develop a writing career, or simply get some additional reward for your expertise.

SAP HANA Cookbook

ISBN: 978-1-78217-762-3   Paperback: 284 pages

Your all-inclusive guide to understanding SAP HANA with practical recipes

1. Understand the architecture of SAP HANA, effectively transforming your business with the modeler and in-memory computing engine.

2. Learn about Business Intelligence, Analytics, and Predictive analytics on top of SAP HANA Models.

3. Gain knowledge on the process of transforming your data to insightful information using the Modeler.

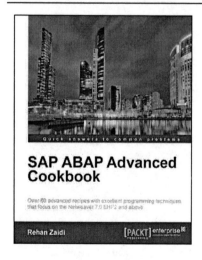

SAP ABAP Advanced Cookbook

ISBN: 978-1-84968-488-0   Paperback: 316 pages

Over 80 advanced recipes with excellent programming techniques that focus on the Netweaver 7.0 EHP2 and above

1. Full of illustrations, diagrams, and tips with clear step-by-step instructions and real time examples.

2. Get to grips with solving complicated problems using Regular Expressions in ABAP.

3. Master the creation of common Design Patterns using ABAP Objects.

4. Enhance SAP applications through the use of ABAP programming.

Please check **www.PacktPub.com** for information on our titles

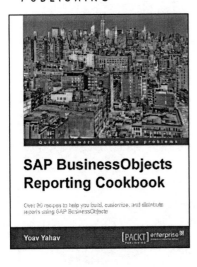

SAP BusinessObjects Reporting Cookbook

ISBN: 978-1-78217-243-7   Paperback: 380 pages

Over 80 recipes to help you build, customize, and distribute reports using SAP BusinessObjects

1. Discover how to master different business solutions which will help you deliver high quality reports to your organization and clients.

2. Work efficiently in a BI environment while keeping your data accurate, secured, and easily shared.

3. Learn how to build and format reports that will enable you to get the most useful insights from your data.

SAP HCM - A Complete Tutorial

ISBN: 978-1-78217-220-8   Paperback: 380 pages

Deploy and implement the diverse functionalities of SAP HCM

1. Delve into the SAP HCM system and the multitude of features it provides.

2. Explore the various infotypes related to numerous business processes in order to manage human resources better.

3. A practical guide filled with real life scenarios, screenshots, and useful tips and tricks.

Please check **www.PacktPub.com** for information on our titles

CPSIA information can be obtained
at www.ICGtesting.com
Printed in the USA
FSOW02n2043020616
21108FS

9 781785 281815